The Education of Dual Sensory Impaired Children: Recognising and Developing Ability

Edited by
David Etheridge

David Fulton Publishers
London

David Fulton Publishers Ltd
2 Barbon Close, London WC1N 3JX

First published in Great Britain by
David Fulton Publishers 1995

HV
1597.2
.E36
1995

British Library Cataloguing in Publication Data

A catalogue record for this book is available from the British Library

ISBN 1-85346-335-3

Typeset by Harrington & Co.
Printed in Great Britain by The Cromwell Press, Melksham.

Contents

List of Abbreviations   v

Contributors to this Book   vi

Foreword by Jessica Hills   vii

Introduction Recognising and Developing Ability   ix
       David Etheridge

Chapter 1   Educational Assessment of Deafblind Learners   1
       Stuart Aitken

Chapter 2   Rebound Therapy as a Method of Developing and
       Assessing Communication   18
       Ruth Farrow

Chapter 3   Objects of Reference   34
       Marion McLarty

Chapter 4   Multi-Sensory Rooms and Dual Sensory Impairment:
       Use and Design   46
       Richard Hirstwood

Chapter 5   The Educational Benefits of Reflexology for Children
       with Dual Sensory Impairments   61
       Sylvia Povey and David Etheridge

Chapter 6   Working with Families of Dual Sensory Impaired
       Children: a Professional Perspective   75
       June Allen

iv

Chapter 7   The Training and Role of Intervenors in One
             Region of Britain   91
             Jonathan Griffiths

Chapter 8   A Consortium Approach to Staff Development   103
             John Kaye and Keith Humphreys

Chapter 9   Coals to Newcastle: Enriching and Extending
             Educational Provision Through Regionalisation   115
             David Etheridge

List of Abbreviations

BSL	British Sign Language
DES	Department of Education and Science
DFE	Department for Education
DHSS	Department of Health and Social Security
GEST	Grant for Educational Support and Training
GEST 29 (14)	Educational Provision for Deaf-Blind Children
INSET	In-Service Training
LEA	Local Education Authority
MSI	Multi-Sensory Impaired
NVQ	National Vocational Qualification
OFSTED	Office for Standards in Education
PMLD	Profound and Multiple Learning Difficulties
RNIB	Royal National Institute for the Blind
Sense	National Deafblind and Rubella Association
SLD	Severe Learning Difficulties

Contributors to this Book

DR STUART AITKEN is Research Fellow at the CALL Centre of the University of Edinburgh and also Principal Officer (Research and Practice) at Sense Scotland.

JUNE ALLEN is an Advisory Teacher with the North East GEST 29 (14) Consortium Project based at the Regional Advisory and Assessment Centre in Newcastle Upon Tyne.

DR DAVID ETHERIDGE is Project Co-ordinator for the North East GEST 29 (14) Consortium Project based at the Regional Advisory and Assessment Centre in Newcastle Upon Tyne.

RUTH FARROW is an Advisory Teacher with the North East GEST 29 (14) Consortium Project based at the Regional Advisory and Assessment Centre in Newcastle Upon Tyne.

JONATHAN GRIFFITHS is RNIB Adviser for Deafblind Education.

JESSICA HILLS is Chairman of Sense.

RICHARD HIRSTWOOD is a freelance trainer and partner in Greyhirst Training.

KEITH HUMPHREYS is Principal Lecturer in the Department of Education Studies at the University of Northumbria in Newcastle.

JOHN KAYE is Senior Lecturer in the Department of Education Studies at the University of Northumbria in Newcastle.

MARION McLARTY was Headteacher of Carnbooth School, Strathclyde and is now Lecturer in Special Education at the University of Strathclyde.

SYLVIA POVEY is proprietor of the North East School of Reflexology.

Foreword

The recognition that children with both visual and auditory impairments need special ways of assessing and educating them, whether or not they have additional disabilities, has been a long time coming. Some children, it is true, have received special education for 'deafblind' children in special schools and units, and others have been at school somewhere with many dedicated teachers who have done their best to work with them. Many of these children, however, have been thought of principally as having more severe learning difficulties, maybe with other disabilities too. Their specific needs arising from their vision and hearing impairments have not been fully understood.

The DES Policy Statement of 1989, *Educational Provision for Deafblind Children*, brought to the attention of Local Education Authorities the need to identify and re-assess these children. The LEAs were asked to inform the DES how they intended to fulfil the children's educational needs. To support the LEAs in the setting up of services the DES GEST 29/92 initiative, *Educational Provision for Deaf-blind Children*, was agreed and has been in progress for nearly the full three-year term.

The GEST 29 14 initiative is a special grant for the development of services for dual sensory impaired children, including those with additional disabilities. The grant has been important in a number of ways. At the grass roots level the funding has provided opportunities for research and development into a range of different educational approaches that may be appropriate for the very individual needs of these children. Secondly, it has resulted in the development of a range of training courses at different levels of complexity and serving some very different purposes. Thirdly, it has enabled the consortia of LEAs that received funding to research different ways of managing a service for the education of children with very low incidence disabilities.

What is meant by 'deafblind'? Who is included? It should be obvious that a combined vision and hearing loss, even if apparently slight, must have a serious effect on a child's capacity to learn and therefore needs assessment. Extra support should be given according to the assessed need. Additional disabilities compound the problem but do not lessen the need for specific attention to the sight and hearing loss. Definition and clarification are important for identification purposes and are discussed in this book. Assessment is given a very thorough exposition and is crucial as an ongoing, all-encompassing process. A variety of possible aspects of the curriculum are presented, all emphasising the importance of developing relationships which will allow touch and lead to communication. The importance of providing children with order and sequence in their confused world is stressed. It enables children to make choices and begin to control their relationships and environment.

The final chapters of this book look at ways of accessing the curriculum and managing the service. One consortium developed an intervenor service, another developed a regional centre with outreach services. Both involved training of staff. The whole programme has resulted in a great deal of awareness raising of the needs of these children. Much expertise has been gained, building on and making use of the expertise that was available to a small number of these children before the programme started. It is essential that this expertise at all levels should not be lost when the programme ends in March, 1995.

This book of essays on some of the above aspects begins to take on the essential recording and dissemination, exposition and promotion that are now needed to ensure not only the continuation of those services in the consortia funded by the DFE but also the development of similar services across the country.

Jessica Hills, MBE BA, B Phil Ed, Dip Ed of Deaf Children
Chairman of Sense

November 1994

INTRODUCTION

Recognising and Developing Ability

David Etheridge

This book is about ability, not disability. It is about what children *can do* and how they *can progress*. All children have the moral, ethical and legal right to be educated, no matter what barriers society puts in their way because of their physical disabilities. Dual sensory impaired children, like all others, have the right under the Education Reform Act, 1988, to a broadly-based and balanced curriculum that is appropriate to their needs since they, like any children, will not develop educationally unless that curriculum is appropriate to their needs.

This book uses the term 'dual sensory impaired' to include rather than to exclude children who have a dual impairment of sight and hearing, and it attempts to cover aspects of educational provision for the majority of those children. Indeed, it tends to deal with children from birth to about fourteen years old who have a dual impairment of sight and hearing from birth or have acquired it at an early age. It is a weakness of this book that its length does not permit coverage of all children and young people with a dual sensory impairment. There are some, such as children and young people with Usher syndrome, who are not included explicitly because of the age of the onset of the full effects of Usher syndrome. The book also does not address the needs of children and young people who are effectively supported in mainstream education by services for single sensory impairments.

The individual chapters that make up this book do not cover all aspects of the special curriculum for dual sensory impaired children but rather concentrate on some of the main areas: assessment; communication; sensory stimulation; the importance of the family; and ways in which these opportunities can be made available. However, before that curriculum is discussed and the ways in which it can be designed to enable the child to make full and individualised use of it are identified, it is important that the group of children we are referring to is defined. The world of education is very good at creating categories of children and giving them very specific names, particularly within the area of special education. However, it is not good at defining those groupings and then sticking to them.

The children who are the subjects of this book are those with a dual impairment of both distance senses (sight and hearing). For some children this impairment may not be physically caused (i.e. the eye and/or the ear does not have any physical impairment) but rather it is sometimes the result of other factors (e.g. lack of appropriate stimulation leading to a very partial use of sight or hearing). However, whatever the causes, the effects of the combined impairment of both distance senses are potentially severe. McInnes and Treffry (1982) described the effects of a dual sensory impairment as:

> ...not just an 'additive' problem of deafness and blindness: nor is it purely one of communication or perception. Children are unable to utilise their distance senses of vision and hearing to receive non-distorted information. The problem is complex.

Children may:

- lack the ability to communicate with their environment in a meaningful way;

- have a distorted perception of their world;

- lack the ability to anticipate future events or the result of their actions;

- be deprived of many of the most basic extrinsic motivations;

- have medical problems which lead to serious developmental lags;

- be mislabelled as retarded or emotionally disturbed;

- be forced to develop unique learning styles to compensate for their multiple handicaps;

- have extreme difficulty in establishing and maintaining interpersonal relationships.

As Heather Murdoch has observed (1994), a child with an impairment of sight and hearing:

> ...faces enormous difficulties in accessing the social context, and has different modes of perceiving the environment. Senses that sighted people rely on deliver very little or no information. Senses delivering largely redundant information to sighted hearing people

assume much greater importance. The child's perception of the world is different – we cannot assume that it is like our perception with parts missing, but we can safely posit a difference. If this early perception forms the basis for cognitive development, then why should development be assumed to follow the same routes as for sighted hearing children? This is not to argue that development necessarily follows different routes, but to suggest that as yet we have insufficient knowledge to state either premise with confidence.

McInnes and Treffry (1982) point out that many children have potentially useful **residual vision and/or hearing**. However, they must be taught to use this potential and to integrate sensory input from the damaged distance senses with past experience and input from other senses. Until they do that they will often function at a level far below their capabilities.

There is little difference in the minds of most professionals about what key areas are needed for an appropriate educational programme. However, there is dispute over the term used to describe these children. In this book a number of terms have been used. Wyman (1986) entitled her work on the subject *Multiply Handicapped Children* whilst the body of her text discussed the needs of deafblind children. McInnes and Treffry (1982) entitled their work *Deafblind Infants and Children* but then used the term multi-sensory deprived in the body of the text. The most widely used terms to describe children with combined impairments of both distance senses are deafblind and multi-sensory impaired.

The term deafblind is a fascinating one in terms of philology. Precisely how it is written is not generally accepted and the term is variously expressed as deafblind, deaf-blind, deaf blind and deaf/blind. It is interesting that the issue is current enough to justify a paper by Salvatore Lagati during the IAEDB conference in Potsdam (Lagati, 1994) where, as a result of considerable international consultation, he suggested that the term used should be deafblind rather than anything else since 'deafblindness is a condition presenting other difficulties than those caused by deafness and blindness'.

Precisely what range of children is represented by this term is also a matter for discussion. Some (Contact, 1993) have suggested that it is 'an umbrella' term which can include:

the blind and profoundly deaf child;
the blind and severely or partially hearing child;
the partially sighted and profoundly deaf child;
the partially sighted and severely or partially hearing child.

Wyman (1986) has accurately observed that:

There is no clear definition of deaf-blindness that will satisfy all the involved professionals. Equally, there is no one disease or syndrome which can now be described as being the main cause of deaf-blindness.

Dale (1990) has argued that the term deafblind is 'an oversimplification which fails to address the variations in cause, time of onset, relative degree of handicap and additional complications this dual handicap can encompass'. The situation is complicated even more by a broadening of the term in an attempt to be all-embracing in its coverage of 'a heterogeneous group of children who may suffer from varying degrees of visual and hearing impairment, perhaps combined with learning difficulties and physical disabilities which can cause severe communication, developmental and educational problems' (DES, 1989).

Others (Best, 1989) would suggest that the definition should be restricted to children purely with dual impairments of sight and hearing. Indeed, this follows a tradition, established through RNIB and other national providers and expressed in works like McInnes and Treffry, which reached its full cultural value during the rubella outbreak of the 1950s and the 1960s.

Before the rubella vaccination programme began to take effect in the 1980s, rubella (or German measles, as it is more commonly called) was the major known cause of deaf-blindness, but children with congenital rubella syndrome are fortunately no longer being born in the large numbers of the 1950s and 1960s, and much can now be done to help the few cases that occur (Wyman, 1986).

There are certainly many causes of dual sensory impairment, such as Usher syndrome, but the great majority of children who comprise this group have additional learning difficulties and can often be found in provision for children with profound and multiple learning difficulties, severe or moderate learning difficulties and physical difficulties. These are the children who function as dual sensory impaired due to uncorrected, but treatable, visual or hearing problems such as congenital cataracts; children who have an impairment of both distance senses due to pre-natal causes such as cytomegalovirus; children affected by pre-natal genetic causes such as retinitis pigmentosa which in about 25 per cent of cases occurs with an attendant hearing loss, Down's syndrome or CHARGE association (Coloboma, Heart defects, Atresia of the choanae, Retarded growth, Genital hypoplasia, Ear abnormalities and/or deafness); children who experience an impairment of sight and hearing due to peri-natal causes such as prematurity or post-natal causes such as meningitis; and children who have an impairment of one distance sense and are not using the other effectively.

Owing to the complexity of the child's condition and additional disabilities some professionals have preferred to adopt the term 'multi-sensory impaired'. The term multi-sensory impaired is one that is associated with the field of learning difficulties and significantly does not specify the discrete effects of a combined impairment of sight and hearing: it might equally apply to a child with a hearing or visual impairment and additional learning difficulties. The term quite rightly suggests that multi-sensory impaired children have additional learning difficulties which are important in their own right and will have an effect on and will be affected by the dual impairment of both distance senses. Indeed, the term is in many ways more acceptable because it can be used to take a more holistic view of the child. It is important to recognise, however, that the effects of a dual sensory impairment will have serious educational implications for children in their own right, the full effects being influenced by a child's additional disabilities.

So why not join the two terms together and, like the DFE, refer to all children as deafblind, or, as others have done, refer to all children as MSI? One of the main arguments used against this is that for deafblind children the effects of their impairments are caused purely by their dual impairment of sight and hearing whilst with MSI children it is difficult to tell whether this is the result of additional disabilities. Indeed, in some circumstances it is important to be able to distinguish individual groups within such a heterogeneous client group and, as Stuart Aitken points out in the first chapter of this book, the form of assessment used to help children demonstrate their abilities is dependent on the combination and complexity of learning difficulties experienced by that child. Educational provision also needs to take account of this fact and, as David Etheridge suggests in the last chapter of this book, schools for children with severe or moderate learning difficulties, although appropriate for the great majority of children with dual impairment of sight and hearing, are not suitable for children with a straight dual sensory impairment.

An alternative strategy is therefore to use the two terms to apply to two very separate client groups – those without additional learning difficulties (deafblind) and those with additional learning difficulties which are not a result of their dual sensory impairment (MSI). However, as this book demonstrates, many aspects of the curriculum for a deafblind child are equally relevant and necessary for an MSI child and it would be unjust and divisive to exclude a group of children from the benefits of provision because of a difficulty with definition. If a child is dual sensory impaired the effects of that dual sensory impairment will be common to all children and no children. As McInnes and Treffry have suggested (1982), the only common feature for this group of children 'labelled deaf-blind is that they all have some degree of deprivation of the use of their distance senses'.

All children are likely to experience similar difficulties in the areas that McInnes and Treffry have detailed above and it is important that the dialectical effects should be addressed in their own right, and not be diagnostically overlaid by other more obvious learning difficulties. Provision for dual sensory impaired children with additional learning difficulties can learn a great deal from the PMLD and SLD lobby but it is not a replication of that provision and, as Collins has observed (Best, 1994), it is wrong to assume that 'if you are trained to teach generally handicapped children you can serve any such child whether they have sensory deficits or not'. Assessment of dual sensory impaired children with additional learning difficulties is more complex than for deafblind children but it is not impossible, and educational programmes, although having to take into account the effects of other disabilities, can be very similar.

This book has adopted the strategy of using the term dual sensory impaired when referring to children in general with dual impairments of both sight and hearing regardless of their other educational needs. Where a specific sub-group is dealt with, such as deafblind children, where a source has used a specific term, whether accurately or not, or where specific and official names are referred to, that term is used. In the field of education for the visually impaired there was made some years ago a very definite division between blind and partially sighted – an unfortunate position which should be avoided in this field. While it is important to be able to differentiate and enable using these specific terms, it is also important not to be divisive. All children with dual impairments of sight and hearing are individuals who will use their abilities in very different ways – they are both *equal* and *exceptional*.

McInnes and Treffry have nine basic assumptions which form part of the foundation from which they worked:

1. In the absence of proven extreme brain damage the child can be reached and educated to become a contributing member of society.

2. In many cases, some or all of the input systems have been damaged, but the processing mechanism has not.

3. The child's ongoing challenge is the development of an adequate basis for communication with and understanding of the environment.

4. The child has been deprived of many of the basic extrinsic motivational factors necessary for normal development.

5. Some of the child's physical disabilities can be overcome by medical

intervention and time.

6. The child must and can be taught to utilise all of the residual potential in each of the sensory input modalities.

7. The child must have a **reactive environment** which he can comprehend and control.

8. The child must have a programme that extends over twenty-four hours per day, seven days per week, and 365 days per year.

9. Parental involvement is essential.

The first six chapters of this book examine aspects of the curriculum for dual sensory impaired children concentrating on assessment, communication, sensory stimulation and the importance of parents and families in a child's development. Assessment is dealt with in chapter one and, although it specifically addresses assessment of deafblind learners, many of the principles that it deals with are equally applicable to all dual sensory impaired children. Stuart Aitken stresses the importance of assessment being designed to suit the needs of the child. No single assessment or test is ever comprehensive and the form of that assessment should be determined by the needs of the child. It should provide information about personal characteristics, the abilities and disabilities of the child, how that child functions in different environments and the resources that are necessary for that child to function effectively. Assessment should allow for a mix of qualitative and quantitative methods, reflecting a world view that is pluralistic, dynamic and complex, approaching people in a value-oriented way and recognising the inter-relatedness of human activities. In this view, assessment is not something done to a learner at certain stages but a continuous process of evaluation of the relationship between learner goals and performances, the educator, the curriculum and its development, and of the resources available. Assessment is an on-going activity rather than a single or static occurrence and should stress the abilities of the child.

This book assumes that all children have the ability and desire to learn as long as their educational environment suits their particular needs. Dr Aitken identifies the importance of assessing communication and chapter two takes this theme further by looking at rebound therapy as a way of providing positive opportunities for communication, for the child and adults working with that child. Rebound therapy uses the energy created by a series of co-active movement routines on a trampoline. It gives children the opportunity to control their environment and the activity which is taking place through communicating at what ever level is appropriate for them. Ruth Farrow places rebound therapy in the context of communication for dual sensory impaired children and then goes on to examine practical examples of ways in which it can enable children to control their own learning.

Communication through objects of reference is examined by Marion McLarty in chapter three. Objects of reference again stress the importance of individuality in developing communication and this chapter examines ways in which they can be used to internalise structures which allow the child to make sense of and impose order on her/his life. In common with the previous chapters it stresses the importance of the child being an active participant in the learning process through the creation of an educational programme that is meaningful to and appropriate for the child at that particular stage in her/his development. All the chapters in this book are written by practitioners and Marion McLarty examines in detail ways in which communication can be created in the classroom.

Chapters four and five continue with the themes of assessment, communication and the development of individual abilities but this time by looking at sensory stimulation. In chapter four multi-sensory rooms and the ways in which they can be designed and used are examined. Richard Hirstwood suggests that they have tremendous potential for the educational development of the dual sensory impaired child but that they must be based on the abilities and interests of that individual. The same message is given in chapter five. Reflexology is a relatively new educational tool but for children who have difficulty in accessing and interacting with their environments it has tremendous potential in enabling them to locate themselves, to develop relationships at their own rate and in their own ways, and to start to communicate with their world not through the distance senses but through sensory stimulation of the feet. Sylvia Povey and David Etheridge also draw attention to the importance of parents in a child's development and identify some examples of ways in which parents and families can use reflexology to enable the child to become a socially functioning being.

Chapter six takes up this theme and examines parents and families from a professional perspective. Stuart Aitken in chapter one identified the importance of parents in the assessment process and June Allen extends this theme as well as examining the development of educational programmes. She stresses the importance of a holistic educational environment, and the quality of partnership with parents that this demands, from the perspective of the child, the family and the professionals. The chapter also looks at practical ways in which this partnership can be established and developed through talking and listening, observing and demonstrating, working together, the importance of location, the presence of other children and the availability of transport, time and group support.

The remaining three chapters deal not so much with the practical programmes that can enable dual sensory impaired children to demonstrate and develop their abilities but rather with some of the ways in which structures can be put into place to enable this process. All three chapters are based on work that has been undertaken during the recent GEST 29 (14) initiative which has made provision available for deafblind children in England and Wales. Jonathan Griffiths examines the training and role of intervenors as it has been developed in Staffordshire and Hereford & Worcester. The Canadian model has been successfully modified to provide individual support to enable effective communication, the receipt of clear information, to enable the child to take full advantage of learning and social experiences and to gain fuller access to the environment and the schools curriculum. The chapter looks at the appointment, training and evaluation of the work of the intervenors within the Staffordshire-led consortium.

The last two chapters examine the work of another of the eight GEST consortia. Chapter eight deals with the training programmes that have been established for professionals and parents in the North East of England who are involved in the educational development of dual sensory impaired children, while chapter nine examines the model for a regional support service that has been established in that consortium. Both chapters stress the importance of regional provision in supporting small numbers of children with complex needs. They, like chapter seven, also emphasise the importance of continued central funding if the developments created with public money are not to collapse.

Dual sensory impaired children are a low-incidence group within the broader context of special educational needs. This creates difficulties in funding, difficulties in provision and difficulties for some in justifying dedication of scarce resources. However, what should be borne in mind regarding dual sensory impaired children is their uniqueness and complexity in relation to their abilities. Rather than justifying reduction in resources and interest, this should create even greater concentration on their development as individuals and their rights to be considered as such. It is easy to ignore minorities, to emphasise problems and emphasise disability. What this book does is no more than many educationalists throughout the world are doing – and might be seen by some as the aim of education – it demonstrates some of the ways in which individual children can demonstrate and develop their individual abilities. After all, dual sensory impaired children have a world to win.

References

Best, A.B. (1989) *Deafblind Education – Developing and sustaining appropriate provision. Proceedings of the International Conference on Deafblind Education.* Birmingham: IAEDB.

Best, A. (1994) 'Trends in policy and practice in deafblind services', in Pape, F.W. (ed) *Access to cultur III. Proceedings of the European Conference of the International Association for the Education of Deafblind People.* Potsdam: IAEDB.

Contact (1993) *A resource for staff working with children who are deaf and blind.* Edinburgh: Moray House.

Dale, F.J. (1990) *The Stimulation Guide.* Cambridge: Woodhead-Faulkner.

Department of Education and Science (1989) *Educational Provision for Deaf-blind Children.* London: HMSO.

Lagati, S. (1994) 'A correct name and a clear definition', in Pape, F.W. (ed) *Access to cultur III. Proceedings of the European Conference of the International Association for the Education of Deafblind People.* Potsdam: IAEDB.

McInnes, J.M and Treffry, J.A. (1982; p'back ed. 1993) *Deafblind Infants and Children: A developmental guide.* London: University of Toronto Press.

Murdoch, H. (1994) 'Case study of a deafblind infant', in Pape, F.W. (ed) *Access to cultur III. Proceedings of the European Conference of the International Association for the Education of Deafblind People.* Potsdam: IAEDB.

Wyman, R. (1986) *Multiply Handicapped Children.* London: Souvenir Press.

CHAPTER 1

Educational Assessment of Deafblind Learners

Dr Stuart Aitken

What is needed for useful and accurate assessment of learners who are deafblind? First, agreement is needed about what the term 'deafblind' means. The single greatest obstacle to devising appropriate assessment tools in this field is lack of an accepted definition of 'deafblindness'. Best (1994), amongst others, has argued in favour of a relatively purist position in defining deafblindness. He argues that the term should be used only if a learner has no additional disabilities, when impairments occur solely to sight and hearing. Others have argued that the term should encompass learners with vision and/or hearing impairment, irrespective of other impairments (e.g. learning disabilities, speech and language disorder).

It is outside the scope of this article to enter into this debate, important though it is for philosophical, conceptual and practical reasons. It is also outside the scope of this article to suggest *why* there is no agreement (see Ennals, 1993). But it *is* useful to know why a working definition of the term deafblindness is an important pre-requisite to assessing those described as deafblind. Suppose the definition is 'all-encompassing'. Suppose too that assessment results are available and they indicate a learner has almost no responses. What does this tell us? It tells us nothing about the underlying reasons for lack of response. Perhaps it was due to sensory impairment; to physical impairment; learning disabilities; lack of experience; unwillingness to cooperate. Or to all of these. If our definition of deafblindness is restricted and refers only to those with impairment both of sight and hearing we can be more confident that lack of response is due to the effects of the dual sensory impairment – and not to the presence of additional disabilities. Table 1.1 shows how different definitions or sub-groups of 'deafblindness' are often associated with different objective assessment instruments.

'Type' of deafblind	Assessment schedule	Areas covered	Teaching suggestions included?
Congenital deafblind	Stillman (1976)	Mostly symbolic communication activities, receptive communication	Not originally (but see Dale)
	Dale (1972)	Similar to Callier-Azusa	Not originally but Dale (1990) covers suggestions which apply to Callier-Azusa and Progress Guide
	Stremel and Wilson (1990)	Communication as main focus but links together physical, sensory, learning abilities	Yes (also trainer's manual). Slightly unusual focus of augmentative communciation
	Tobin and Myers (1978)	Short-term memory (for its importance in areas such as communication and sequencing)	No
	van Dijk (1971)	Cognitive and communication	Not directly
	Best *et al* (1979)	Early communication behaviour – up to the first sign	No
	McInnes and Treffry (1982)	Developmental guide for deafblind infants and children	Most of focus on teaching but includes assessments in context
	van Dijk (1982)	Book includes observational checklists and complements Denver Developmental Screening Test	No
	Contact (1991)	Not explicitly assessment manual	Embedded within teaching guide

'Type' of deafblind	Assessment schedule	Areas covered	Teaching suggestions included?
Late onset deafblind e.g. Usher			
Visual and multiple disability	Aitken and Buultjens (1992)	Mostly concentrating on assessing functional vision	Yes
	British adaptation by Sebba (1978)	For observing and recording visual responses	Differs from above in not linking training suggestions but information can be used in this way
Deafblind and multiple disability	Rudolph et al (1975)	Communication plus other areas	No
	Donlon and Curtis (1972)	Uses video in assessing number of areas	No
Hearing and additional disability	Murdoch (1994)	Functional hearing assessment for learners with additional disabilities	No
Severe disability	Kiernan and Jones (1977)	Areas such as looking, listening and touching – set out in developmental sequence	Basis for planning educational objectives
	Keirnan and Read(1987)	Communication – good basis but needs to be adapted if using with sensory loss	No but links in to related publication

Table 1.1 Relation between definitions of deafblindness and example assessment instruments

Table 1.1 gives a flavour of different approaches that may be taken, depending in part on which definition of 'deafblindness' is thought appropriate by service providers. No single assessment or test is ever comprehensive: for instance, none of those listed in the table address emotional development or social interaction (though they may do so through their teaching suggestions, where appropriate). Nor does any one of them give rise to the possibility that deafblindness may be accompanied by 'dyslexia type' problems, e.g. reading problems as a third factor rather than as secondary effect of the impairment of both distance senses.

WHAT IS ASSESSMENT FOR?

Assume for a moment that a definition of deafblindness is agreed (international agreement on a new descriptor – 'deafblind' replacing 'deaf-blind' – is not the same as agreement on what the descriptor refers to) and is applied only to learners who have both sight and hearing impairments. Are we now in a position to develop assessment instruments in which we will have full confidence? To put it another way, are the formal assessment instruments described in Table 1.1 comprehensive enough? The answer is only partially yes. Much depends on the purpose behind assessment. Table 1.2 shows some of the different aims for assessment.

Purpose of assessment	Rationale
Establish a baseline	– identify strengths and weaknesses – agree learner performance – compare learners
Re-assess to record change	– identify performance in different areas of activity – compare change in areas of curriculum targeted against those not: shows effective education
Ascertain teaching steps	– next steps in assessment may indicate next steps to take with learner
Suggest learning or curriculum objectives	– some assessment procedures give specific suggestions

Table 1.2 Purposes of educational assessment

The fact that there are different purposes to assessment is one reason why it is not possible to agree on 'the most appropriate assessment to carry out'. Different people may have quite different expectations of the role of assessment. Within education the purpose might be early identification, screening, prediction of performance, establishing whether a learner's performance deviates from the norm or for some other reason. Assessment has many similarities to reading a map: if I want to get to London by car I will use a map with a scale of perhaps 1 inch to 5 miles; but if I want to go hill-walking this sort of scale would be of little use.

Even when used to address precisely the same question of the same learner, different assessment tools may well result in different answers. In which one are we to have confidence? Two direct analogies demonstrate this problem:

1. When assessing a learner's vision, practitioners from different disciplines often rely on different methods. An ophthalmologist may use objective techniques. An orthoptist may require the learner's co-operation, and hence use subjective techniques. A teacher or parent may rely on observing the learner in natural settings using measures of functional vision (some use the term behavioural measures). Examples of each of these approaches are shown in Table 1.3.

Objective tests	Subjective tests	Behavioural techniques, e.g.
Ophthalmoscopy	STYCAR	Natural observation
Eye position, spontaneous movement	BUST	Vision for Doing
Reflexes	LH	Look and Think
Blinking	Illiterate E	
OKN	Landholt's rings	
ERG	Ffook's Test	
VEP	Figures/symbol charts	
'Refraction'	Letter charts, reading charts, reading passages	

Table 1.3 Different approaches to assessing vision

Which is right? The answer depends on what you want to know. If the purpose is diagnosis, prognosis, monitoring deterioration, then it is essential to use objective methods. If, however, the emphasis is to make use of available sight, then behavioural or functional measures will be to the fore. Other circumstances warrant use of subjective measures. Each is appropriate, none on its own is enough to provide a complete picture of the learner.

2. Even within any one approach to assessing vision different results may emerge. This is shown in Table 1.4, in which different techniques of visual assessment, all of which are 'objective', are shown to have slightly different emphases.

	Visual evoked potential	Preferential looking	Optokinetic nystagmus
Each technique depends on different kind of response	Records activity of occipital cortex	Depends on behavioural response	Both visual and motor responses requiring intact visual system and eye movement pathways
Each uses different stimuli	Uses on/offs for flashes, stripes, checkerboards or patterns	Uses stationary patterns – mostly stripes but can also use diagonal, vertical or horizontal stripes and stepped patterns (Vernier acuities)	Uses moving stripes and patterns
Visual acuity thresholds measured by each test use different criteria			

Table 1.4 Comparison of features of three types of 'objective' tests of vision. Three different measures each with different aims, techniques and, potentially, results

Assessment pluralism should be reflected throughout a deafblind learner's life. At school, fine-grained observational analysis may be necessary to work out the extent, content, precursors and consequences of challenging behaviour. For young learners, it may be essential to detect and analyse the sequence of reciprocal movements of the learner and educator in order to structure a precise movement and interaction curriculum. Observational tools are available to make life easier at each and every level of assessment. For instance Odor (1994) has produced a Sequence Analyser to reduce the time taken to analyse video materials. Using it, the educator can encode behavioural events, leaving the computer to analyse links between learner and educator behaviours.

Two of the most common categories of formal assessment tools in use within education are those which are norm-referenced and criterion-referenced. We consider these in a little more detail below. Having done so we set out the contribution that can be made by functional assessment approaches. Finally, in this section, we bring together these approaches, integrating them into what we believe should be the basis of any comprehensive assessment.

Norm-referenced assessment: a political context

When assessment is norm-referenced, that is, based on a 'sample population', assessment can become testing. Results may then indicate if the learner's performance deviates from the norm. A norm is a normal or average performance as devised from a standard sample of the population. Any norm is restricted to the particular population from which it was derived.

National Testing is one example of norm-referenced testing – at least it would be if it had first been standardised on a sample population: but it wasn't, so it isn't! If National Testing is eventually derived from a sample of the population but that sample does not include learners drawn from a particular group – for instance deafblind learners – the results of that National Test may not be applicable to that group (if items have never been tested on any sample of the population then it does not apply to any of the population). Norm-referenced testing must be representative of the population under consideration. There is, though, a ready cop-out. By stating that the National Curriculum (or 5-14 Curriculum in Scotland) is truly a *curriculum for all*, it can be argued (with political, but not with scientific justification) that National Testing must also be applicable to all. In this view National Testing fulfils the criteria of testing what is supposedly being learned, i.e. the National Curriculum. This politicisation of assessment and testing is a real phenomenon.

Norm-referenced assessment and testing can become a tool for establishing and maintaining power and relationships in society. Hanson (1994) argues that assessment through testing has become a major force in exerting power. Zola (1984) pointed out that assessment procedures and rehabilitative programmes reflect value systems. Willard (1982) too has argued that learner's needs are not facts about people, but personal goals and things or activities valued by people. For learners who have special educational needs the usefulness of testing can be suspect, and their accuracy often questionable. It is right to remain sceptical and suspicious of this type of assessment and testing. When applied to learners who have special educational needs tests do not in themselves increase equality and effectiveness in society. But norm-referenced testing is not the only way to carry out assessment.

Criterion-referenced assessment: an easier option?

In some circumstances criterion-referenced approaches have advantages over those which are norm-referenced. Close and explicit association between assessment and learning objectives allows for fine tuning of observational skills. The aim is not to place the learner along some sort of continuum but to establish the standard or criterion to be aimed at. Or so the distinction would seem. But under the surface of criterion-referenced testing there are assumptions about what constitutes 'normal' child development – what Tobin (1994) calls an 'internal checklist', drawn from the educator's experience.

Although criterion-referenced instruments have advantages they can also present problems of their own. The fact that they are:

- relatively easy to produce

- can require little in the way of validation

- allow the designer to 'make his or her mark' with the new assessment, and

- require little in the way of statistical knowledge to interpret

may have led to a proliferation of new criterion-referenced assessments. This is not to argue that all criterion-referenced assessments are poor – many are indeed excellent – merely that they should be used with caution.

When applying so-called objective methods of assessment – be they standardised scores or criterion-referenced skills – it should be remembered that item selection makes certain assumptions about what is and is not important. There is one reason for exercising caution in applying and interpreting assessment schedules borrowed from other domains, e.g. Portage (Boyd & Bluma, 1977). One of the problems with instruments such as this is that few have been designed and standardised for visually impaired people or hearing impaired people – far less for deafblind learners. Tobin (1994) addresses this point, arguing the need 'to interpret with care results that have not been standardised on a population of visually handicapped children'. Not only is Tobin's statement true for visual impairment, the general principle applies also to deafblindness.

Norm- and criterion-referenced forms of assessment are rather narrow and formal in their application, depending on checklists, developmental scales and so on. There is a place for observational assessment, with the educator observing behaviours, interpreting these in the light of other knowledge about this and other learners, and determining educational objectives. Rigid adherence to objective assessments, without parallel application and enhancement of observational skills, will achieve little. Sole reliance on objective assessment and testing in deafblindness can be very misleading. To take an example: in the early development of deafblind children the focus of learning is usually primarily in the development of interaction and communication skills. Unless the educator is prepared to respond to the learner in a way that is appropriate and in context it is unlikely that the learner will perceive the educator to be a good communication partner. Ascertaining the right way to respond to the learner demands of the educator an ability to pick up on the subtlest of cues – based on the learner's response, environmental cues, past history and responses of other important communicating partners. None of this knowledge comes from any checklist or objective assessment, no matter how detailed.

Functional assessment approaches

Instead of abstracting tasks from settings, functional assessment tries to structure the environment to offer opportunities for observing skills in practical use. Functional assessment approaches assume it is not possible to prescribe for each and every possible situation that may arise with a learner. There is no single correct answer or indeed question.

Elements of functional assessment

Functional assessment should certainly include assessment of the learner's own constellation of abilities and disabilities: cognitive abilities, sensory and perceptual abilities; memory, planning, learning and problem solving; communicative abilities. For the purposes of education, play and therapy these would all be important features of information gathering. But these would not be the only things of interest.

In addition to knowing about personal characteristics, abilities and disabilities, we will want to know how the learner functions in different environments. These would include classroom, home, in the park and other settings. If the learner performs well in one setting, what is it about that setting that acts as an aid? Is it specific to the teacher/carer? Can features of that setting be transferred across to other settings?

Having identified **personal factors** and **environmental factors**, we would want to discover what **resources** are available. These might include a sibling or neighbour, or a particular teacher who is interested in technology. Resources may be of a more formal kind, such as funding or time available for training staff and user.

One extremely important part of any assessment will be to identify which parts of the curriculum lend themselves to incorporating other features. Rather than a learner being a set of parts, aspects of mobility may offer opportunities for communication, for therapy, for play, for problem solving and so on. As part of the process of functional assessment, the assessor takes an active part in identifying these opportunities: they are not contained within artificially constructed categories.

Systems sensitive assessment

Assessment should allow for a mix of qualitative and quantitative methods, reflecting a world view that is pluralistic, dynamic and complex, approaching people in a value-oriented way and recognising the inter-relatedness of human activities. In this view assessment is not something done to a learner at certain stages, but a continuous process of evaluation of the relationship between learner goals and performances, the educator, the curriculum and its development, and of the resources available. Assessment is an on-going activity, rather than a single or static occurrence. Nowhere is this more true than in assessment of communication.

This 'systems led' or 'environment sensitive' approach would include school-centred learning as a focus but would be more than this, encompassing the individual's learning across any setting. In this view assessment cannot be reified and placed 'outside' of the learner and his or her world, or outside of the experiences of assessors. The acts of completing checklists, scales or protocols – helping to clarify areas for further observation – are not themselves 'the assessment'. Instead they are merely tools used during the process of assessment (Millar *et al*, 1986).

Assessment must consider the learning setting, attitudes of staff, training and information needs, and not just reflect a narrow focus on the individual learner. To take an example of the importance of having information on these areas: learners may have apparently adequate systems of communicating but may use these systems only within an educational setting, avoiding their use in personal interaction. Kraat (1985) and Harris (1982) have shown how barriers to interaction can arise between non-speakers and untrained partners. Despite their research having been carried out within the augmentative communication field, their conclusions can be applied to those communicating with deafblind learners. These barriers include:

- domination of conversation (not yielding)

- assumption of user's intellectual level

- misinterpreting intended messages

- inadequate waiting time

- interruptions during waiting times.

There is little point in laying any of these 'inabilities' at the learner's door: the examples in this list are all things the communication partner can do something about, given the will to do so. Unless and until assessment procedures incorporate, as a matter of course, analysis of these and other variables, answers returned may well be misleading. Educationalists often criticise our medical colleagues for adopting a narrow medical-model, within-person view of assessment. We cannot make this criticism while repeating the mistake by developing assessment instruments that have within-person factors as their sole focus.

WISH LIST FOR ASSESSMENT

In the previous section we identified some of the pros and cons of different assessment approaches and touched on the advantages of an integrated 'systems sensitive approach'. It is time now to set out our stall. In this section we bring together those issues of definition, of assessment purpose we have been discussing, and set them within a systems-sensitive approach. We conclude by considering how this or any other approach to assessment could be made more fit for public consumption. First, what mechanism could make this all happen?

Developing an assessment instrument: a role for GEST?

One way to overcome the difficulties presented by definition of deafblindness, and by multiple purposes of assessment, is to carry out a *post hoc* analysis of a very large database of learner information. As a result of the GEST 29 (14) initiative we are now well placed to *begin* to establish a useful assessment instrument. To do so for a low incidence disability will require a multi-centre approach with practitioners co-operating to produce a single (or several) instruments. The GEST initiative could contribute significantly to the education of deafblind children if results are collated from all participating members of every single consortium. In order that this collation be done in a meaningful way, agreement will have to be reached about definition, assessment criteria, methodologies used, and how to interpret results. If done in this way it would not matter that some authorities chose to focus on 'purist deafblind' while others chose a more all-embracing group. The analysis could reflect this heterogeneity. Such an exercise could be carried out in an evaluation of the GEST initiative.

In the following section we consider in a little more depth what the outcome might look like. We develop this framework in an holistic setting: a sort of checklist of what is needed in assessment.

A framework for assessment

Assessment aims

Assessment would be a cyclical process: once the cycle is gone round once, the next cycle begins. As well as early decisions about

- the disabling effects of sensory, physical and other impairments (and remaining abilities);

- the problems and possibilities of communicating

- appropriate steps to take on first contact, and

- follow up activities

we need continued information, reviewing

- the changing abilities and development of the learner (and the effect of this on approaches to communication and other areas)

- changes in environment (e.g. effects of a new staff member as key worker)

and investigating the 'environment' through

- effects on learner, parents and siblings as a result of curricular changes

- resources available (in school, or skills available through other staff members)

in order to adjust our approaches.

Some of the skills required in this broader description of assessment depend on skilled observation of the learner, others are people skills required of the assessor – e.g. picking up on a parent's hidden message. To help avoid activities becoming stuck, tools should cover a range of planning, observation, and analysis as part of assessment.

Dimensions of assessment

We need to be able to assess change in abilities and behaviour, understand why changes are happening, and promote those which are beneficial. To do this we need to monitor both long-term changes and the processes which cause or are associated with such changes. Therefore records need to be kept of

- initial behaviours and abilities, reviewing these measures at regular intervals

- short time-scale behaviours relating to critical skills

- long time-scale processes.

We also need to identify links between our observations and our stated aims and objectives, noting

- the relationship between recorded aspects and aims and goals.

Analysis of these so-called 'within-person' factors, though necessary, is not sufficient. The learner's environment often plays an important part. A major aspect of that environment is the behaviour of staff themselves. The role of the school or other establishment needs to be monitored just as much as the behaviours of the learner. Our final assessment dimension is therefore

- long term processes in the school or other centre, including how resources are allocated; staff attitudes, behaviours and skills.

Assessment tools

Assessment tools could meet the above assessment demands through

1. *Initial profile and statement of aims and objectives* This contributes to the work of defining individual needs and establishing the curriculum. The profile should make as much use as possible of existing evidence available through medical and school records, and recognise the crucial role played by family members – the main source of information on a learner. In order to help this process, inter-agency collaboration is required right from the start with the learner central to these discussions. A video record of the learner in school and/or home may be helpful but only if agreed by all parties.

2. *Personal diaries, or other records* These contribute both to short- and long-term process measures, and to monitoring our own effectiveness. Diaries and log sheets need not be complicated to be useful: often simple extensions to records already kept will be fine.

3. *Video records, together with informal and formal analysis of video transcripts* Video records are useful in two distinct ways. First, they can be a valuable focus for after-the-event review by staff of significant sessions, as well as a reminder of how the learner was prior to intervention. Second, they allow objective analysis to be carried out of critical behaviours: for instance, initiations, appropriate responses, and so on. Minute or micro-analysis of video sequences can be useful for advising co-workers of more appropriate response patterns: but too much of it and it is unlikely ever to be analysed.

4. *Review profile* Similar in form to the initial profile, this helps generate an overview of gains over an extended period. Each at-a-glance review profile is unique to the individual and has to be tailored to suit individual needs.

Different views: different information

Different people often have different views of events in a learner's development. Although the assessment tools above are designed to be as objective as possible, many results are based on subjective judgements, which in turn rest on people's different perceptions. A useful technique, and one which can be built into all assessment procedures, is that of triangulation. Multiple evidence can be gathered about the same event, with the intention of reaching, if not a consensus, at least the most likely interpretation.

There will inevitably be differences. It is not necessary to resolve them in an abstract way: one of the strengths of functional assessment is the ability to set up experiences which provide just those observational opportunities needed to determine actual abilities. Profile discrepancies become translated into intervention plans, but with the priority shifted away from development of the learner into informing the staff.

This 'assessment wish list' can and should be augmented by formal assessment instruments, but only where appropriate. There can never be a prescription for exactly when and in what circumstances to do so. Bearing in mind that such formal tools may not have been standardised on a deafblind population, they can still offer clues as to the ways ahead with the individual learner.

WHO IS ASSESSMENT FOR: A PASSPORT TO THE FUTURE?

It is not enough that the results of assessment are kept private. The current fragmentation of piecemeal records held across countless centres and agencies (different records are often held by several different practitioners in education, plus others in social services, health and so on) leads to people becoming fragments, serving the purpose of the agency, rather than the opposite. Indeed, even if the suggestions contained in the previous section were to be taken up, it is likely that the documentation, procedures and outcomes would continue to be aimed at this 'select few'.

Is there a way around this? Results could and should be released to the family and other interested parties in a form that is useful and relevant to the learner's own needs (with confidentiality of the family respected). One interesting way of tackling this has been taken by Sally Millar (Millar & McEwen, 1993). The Personal Passport brings together essential information about the learner – from detailed medical reports, formal assessments, confidential case-notes, facts stored in people's heads – and turns it into a form readily accessible to anyone. Crucially the passport is the learner's property, written in a highly personal style, and he or she holds the power of that knowledge. A passport 'saves endless repetition by parents/carers; may cut down distressing or frustrating incidents; hasten the development of positive relationships; ensure consistent management, and smooth the integration of new staff working with a client' (Millar & McEwen, 1993). Through this the results of assessment become the property of the learner.

References

Aitken, S. and Buultjens, M. (1992) *Vision for Doing: Assessing functional vision of learners who are multiply disabled.* Edinburgh: Moray House.

Best, A. B. *et al.* (1979) *Schedule of Communication Development in Deaf-Blind Children.* London: NADBRH.

Best, A. B. (1989) *Deafblind Education – Developing and sustaining appropriate·provision. Proceedings of the International Conference on Deafblind Education.* Birmingham: IADB.

Best, A. B. (1994) 'Deafblind Education – Developing and sustaining appropriate provision'. Paper presented at Conference on Deafblind Education, University of Aston, Birmingham, 23rd March.

Boyd, R. D. and Bluma, S. M. (1977) *Portage Parent Program.* Wisconsin: Cooperative Education Service Agency.

Contact (1991) *A resource for staff working with children who are deaf and blind.* Edinburgh: Moray House.

Dale, F. J. (1972) *Progress Guide for Deaf-blind and Severely Handicapped Children.* London: NADBRH.

Dale, F. J. (1990) *The Stimulation Guide.* Cambridge: Woodhead-Faulkner.

Donlon, E. T. and Curtis, W.S. (1972) *The development and evaluation of a video-taped protocol for the examination of multi-handicapped deaf/blind children*. New York: Syracuse University.

Ennals, P. (1993) 'The Emperor's New Clothes – The World of Deafblindness'. Paper presented at Sense Scotland Conference, Dundee, 17th-19th September.

Hanson, F. A. (1994) *Testing: Social consequences of examined life.* Berkeley: University of California Press.

Harris, D. (1982) 'Communication interaction processes involving non-vocal physically handicapped children', *Topics in Language Disorders*, **2** (2), 21–37.

Kiernan, C. and Jones, M. (1977) *Behaviour Assessment Battery.* Windsor: NFER-Nelson.

Kiernan, C. and Reid, B. (1987) *Pre-verbal Communication Schedule.* Windsor: NFER-Nelson.

Kraat, A. (1985) *Communication interaction between aided and natural speakers. A State of the Art Report.* Toronto: Canadian Rehabilitation Council for the Disabled.

McInnes, J. M. and Treffry, J.A. (1982) *Deafblind Infants and Children: A Developmental Guide.* London: University of Toronto Press.

Millar, S. and McEwen, G. (1993) 'Passports to Communication', in A.Wilson and S.Millar (eds) *Augmentative Communication in Practice: Scotland Collected Papers Study Day.* Edinburgh: CALL Centre.

Millar, S., Nisbet, P. D., Odor, J. P., and Milne, M. (1986) *Communication aids and computer based learning: assessment techniques and related developments for communication impaired learners.* Edinburgh: CALL Centre.

Murdoch, H. (1994) 'Assessing functional hearing'. Paper presented at Sense Scotland Conference, Dundee, 17th-19th September.

Odor, J. P. (1994) *Sequence View.* Edinburgh: CALL Centre.

Rudolph, J.M., Bjorling, B. J., and Collins, M. T. (1975) *Manual for the Assessment of a Deaf-Blind Multiply-Handicapped Child.* Lansing, Michigan: Mid-West Regional Centre for the Deaf-Blind.

Sebba, J. (1978) A system for assessment and intervention for pre-school profoundly retarded multiply handicapped children. M.Ed. thesis. Manchester: University of Manchester.

Stillman, R. (1976) *Callier-Azusa Scale.* Dallas, USA: Callier Hearing and Speech Centre.

Stremel, K., and Wilson, R. (1990) *Communication systems and routines: a decision making process.* Hattiesburg: University of Southern Mississippi.

Tobin, M. J. (1994) *Measuring Visually Impaired People: An Introduction to Test Procedures.* London: Fulton.

Tobin, M. J., and Myers, S. O. (1978) *Memory Span Tests for the deaf-*

blind. Birmingham: University of Birmingham.

van Dijk, J. (1971) 'Learning difficulties and deaf/blind children', in *Proceedings of the Fourth International Conference on Deaf/Blind Children.* Watertown, Mass: Perkins School for the Blind.

van Dijk, J. (1982) *Rubella Handicapped Children.* London: Swets and Zeitlinger.

Willard, L. D. (1982) 'Needs and medicine', *Journal of Medicine and Philosophy,* **7** (3), 259–274.

Zola, I. K. (1984) 'Disincentives to independent living', in *Proceedings of the 2nd International RESNA Conference.* Ottawa: RESNA.

CHAPTER 2

Rebound Therapy as a Method of Developing and Assessing Communication

Ruth Farrow

Introduction

This chapter looks at the opportunities for communication which can be presented to dual sensory impaired children through rebound therapy. The work described developed firstly from attendance on an advance rebound therapy course, and secondly from observing and working with a seven year old dual sensory impaired girl with severe learning difficulties during her weekly rebound sessions. It very quickly became apparent that rebound therapy gave very positive opportunities for communication both to the child and to the adults working with her.

It seemed appropriate therefore to investigate the potential of rebound therapy for developing and assessing communication with dual sensory impaired children. I was able to do this in my capacity as an Advisory Teacher with a GEST 29 (14) project, by observing rebound therapy sessions with a range of children and staff in a variety of special schools in the North East of England, in addition to involvement in weekly rebound therapy sessions over a period of six months.

Most children integrate themselves into their environment by a process of reflex reaction to the world around them. The child reaches out to explore the external environment and the process of establishing body awareness proceeds automatically. In all of this the senses play an essential part. Touch, sight, sound, taste and smell come together to enable the child to make sense of the outside world and to become at home in it. All this usually happens without the adult making a conscious contribution to these processes.

If, however, these earlier proprioceptive experiences have been prevented, by brain injury for example, another way of stimulating the sensory system must be found in order that the development of body image and spatial awareness can take place.

> Children need to discover how their bodies move in order to distinguish one part of their body from another. (Stewart, 1990)

David Stewart goes on to emphasise that good body image is an essential requirement in order to have a sound base upon which to build perceptual skills. If children have good body image, spatial awareness and balance, their bodies can act in an integrated manner.

Body image is a variable concept but Cratty (1979) states that it includes:

> the responses the child makes relative to his/her body's shape, size, components, and perceived capacity for movement and interaction with the environment.

Cratty also suggests that movement is a vital factor if a child with learning difficulties and sensory impairments is going to be given the maximum opportunity to develop cognitively.

Sherborne (1979) worked with children who had severe learning difficulties and observed that:

> Children with severe handicaps would appear to have two prerequisites for making significant progress:
> a) a need to improve their self-awareness and body image
> b) a need to develop an awareness of others through the ability to make meaningful relationships.

Sherborne developed a movement method which enabled these two prerequisites to take place. Rebound therapy develops these equally well.

> The rebound therapy system offers an easy way of flooding
> the child's senses of touch and spatial awareness in a controlled,
> safe system, and the trampoline bed became our earliest working
> tool. (Williams, 1984)

Deryck Williams was referring to a system of movement on the trampoline which was developed by Eddy Anderson, who at the time was head teacher at a special school in Cleveland. Anderson used the energy freely available from the trampoline bed to generate a system of movement which used this easily released and controlled kinetic force.

Anderson (1987) continually emphasises that this is *not* trampolining. Adults operating rebound therapy must be aware when a child is transferring from rebound to trampolining so that the child's needs are met safely and sensibly and fall within the requirements of the British Trampolining Federation.

Anderson was looking for a structured environment which provided a dynamic situation which could be used daily in order to provide for children with profound and multiple learning disabilities. He wanted an environment which facilitated a multi-sensory approach, e.g. one which provided sensori-motor input, and auditory and visual stimuli which awakened or facilitated basic body reflexes, body image, and spatial awareness. Rebound therapy has not been devised to develop skill learning as an end in itself but to develop problem solving, concept formation and sequential thinking. 'The simple activity of bouncing on the trampoline teaches the child a great deal about his (*sic*) own body. It enables him to become more aware of the position of his body in space as well as the relationship between body parts.' (Young, 1986)

Whilst working on the trampoline the child and the adult have to develop a one-to-one working relationship, social interaction and communication skills. A major advantage of rebound therapy is that it is fun and both the child and the adult can gain pleasure and fitness from the activity.

Rebound therapy is a very dynamic system. Apart from the opportunities to develop body image and spatial awareness there are other significant educational aspects to this work, e.g:

• development of relationships

• opportunities for communication

• development of advocacy.

The length of this chapter does not allow for a detailed description of the safety aspects or the techniques used but many of these will be discussed in a later section.

Communication functions

This study concentrates on the following communication functions

• satisfaction of needs

• control of the environment

• regulating interpersonal interaction

as these would seem to be the functions most appropriate to the needs of children with profound learning disabilities and additional sensory impairments.

'Somehow, we have to ensure that children want to communicate, that there is someone to communicate with, that they have something to communicate about and that we teach them that communication is enjoyable and brings results.' (Mittler, 1988) Peter Mittler goes on to question:

How often do we present each child with opportunities for choice and decision making?
How many adult child interactions are initiated by the child?
Who responds and how?
What happens as a result?
How can we help a child to learn that initiations of interaction are rewarding and lead to desired outcomes?

Rebound therapy can provide opportunities and situations in which these questions can be answered.

Coupe and Goldbart (1988) suggest that behaviours are exhibited to both internal and external stimuli which are received through all sensory channels. At this level, any behaviour which indicates a change from a previous state can be interpreted as a signal by an adult. Ouvry (1987) suggests that children need to be able to produce behaviours which are consistent and which can therefore be accurately interpreted by others. Children move from the pre-intentional stage of communication when they begin to realise that facial, vocal, gestural and other behaviours may have an effect on people around them and that they can begin to communicate their needs. By creating situations for this development to take place some children can be encouraged to develop early intentional communication. Coupe and Goldbart (1988) state that 'this stage must be deliberately taught and carefully structured'. This can be achieved by using rebound therapy as the 'carefully structured' situation.

Communication is inherent in every activity undertaken with the children and the establishment of some form of interaction is an essential pre-requisite for teaching. Communication is also vital for the personal development of the children as it allows them to express and to satisfy their physical needs, their need for social interaction and their need for understanding and organising their surroundings. (Ouvry, 1987)

Rebound therapy fulfils these three functions and gives opportunities for children to develop their communication skills whatever their level of functioning might be.

Moody (1986) worked with older learning disabled children and looked at the area of non-verbal communication. He found that whilst working with his students on the trampoline he became much more aware of non-verbal communication taking place especially through facial expression, eye contact, and body contact. He also realised how important facial expression is in communication, as the face is part of the body which is most clearly observed during interaction on the trampoline. The close physical contact involved in movement activities such as rebound therapy encourages synchronisation of action. This is essential for children who must rely on physical clues or co-active signing as their main channel for receptive communication.

For children with profound disabilities in addition to sensory impairment, the system of Total Communication gives them every possible cue that may help them attribute meaning and understanding to the words and actions of others. If a child is working toward vocalising, rebound therapy can assist the physical process.

> The physical basis of speech can be helped in some cases through rebound therapy. The steady rhythm of the bed pushes the abdominal viscera against the diaphragm forcibly expelling air from the lungs across the vocal chords. This explosive release of air can be the beginning of previously uninformed speech patterns. (Beachill, 1985)

Although not specifically referring to rebound therapy when she put forward these ideas, Wyman exactly describes the focus of this work when writing in general about movement experiences:

> Through the use of movement the child is able to become involved in the interaction process and may begin to anticipate and restart a movement following a pause. He (*sic*) may give some indication which the adult can interpret as a signal to restart an activity. The child may indicate that he has enjoyed the activity by moving his limbs or bouncing on his bottom or pushing the adult or taking the adult's hands and putting them back in the correct position for the movement to be restarted. It is important that this stage is recognised and that the child is encouraged through the adult's response to use movements to effect change. (Wyman, 1986)

As a result of their disabilities dual sensory impaired children receive confused information from the environment which causes them to feel threatened. They have problems making sense of the world and this results in a failure to communicate and an intolerance of external interaction. As a consequence the establishment of emotional and social relationships are delayed and they become locked into themselves, often exhibiting stereotyped behaviour such as finger flicking, eye poking and head banging as a form of self-stimulation. The needs of dual sensory impaired children must therefore be identified in order to provide them with a suitable learning environment and appropriate learning strategies. The environment in which dual sensory impaired children learn must be designed to give them security, familiarity, consistency and structure. They need structured routines where they are given opportunities to make choices, solve problems, and above all, communicate. They need to develop relationships and attachments to people and through these relationships will learn to explore and discover, thus developing their own self-image.

The learning environment provided for a dual sensory impaired child must be a reactive environment. It must allow the child to make choices and solve problems whilst feeling secure. It must encourage the use of residual vision and hearing and it must allow the child to move around safely. The environment must also provide the child with opportunities to develop social and emotional relationships.

Creating a reactive environment for a child is an important step in providing the necessary stimulation for the child to learn. When teaching dual sensory impaired children it is important that they understand the environment in which they are learning by receiving clues as to where they are and what is going to happen next. A reactive environment is designed to allow dual sensory impaired children to have control over their interaction whilst at the same time providing for their needs of love, affection and security.

McInnes and Treffry (1982) state that a reactive environment must include the following features:

- emotional bonding

- problem solving

- utilisation of residual vision and hearing

- communication.

Rebound therapy can provide this reactive environment and can be used as part of a dual sensory impaired child's structured routine. Very few young dual sensory impaired children are motivated to move and they may have little or no knowledge of what their bodies are capable of. Many have very poor body image and one of the aims must be to give them an awareness of where their hands, feet, arms and legs are, and the different ways in which they can move them.

For a dual sensory impaired child the stage of motor development reached often parallels stages of social, emotional, and intellectual development. Motor activities should be planned to provide children with opportunities to learn awareness of themselves and their environment. As well as the development of body image and spatial awareness, rebound therapy can also give the child the opportunity to develop communication skills. 'All behaviour is interpreted as communication. Regardless of the development level, a person is never non-communicative' (Aalborg-skolen, 1991) Visser (1988) suggests that 'signal behaviour is the primary goal of communication development'. Rebound therapy presents opportunities for this signal behaviour to take place. Visser goes on to emphasise how important it is that these early signals are interpreted by adults so that the child learns that his signals can produce a response.

McInnes and Treffry (1982) state that: 'For many MSI children who are functioning at an extremely low level, the simple body signal may be the level of communication at which the child is capable of functioning.'

> Through intensive play activities, it is hoped to establish that the child's own body is giving good messages, that these messages are received by the adult and that they will be modified or extended according to the child's needs. (Wyman, 1986)

This observation from Rosalind Wyman describes the focus of this study. Although she was referring to activities in general, the comment can be directly related to rebound therapy.

Case studies

Over a period of six months, regular weekly observations were made of one child in detail. Two further groups of children were observed, each on two occasions. Video recordings were made wherever possible and field notes were taken to document the observations made. Observations were made on the following areas:

- opportunities for the adult to communicate with the child
- opportunities for the child to communicate with adult.

During the sixth month period, observations were made of one rebound session per week with a seven year old girl with a dual sensory impairment. Sarah has moderate hearing loss in both ears and has optic nerve hypoplasia with a converging squint. She also has severe learning difficulties. Sarah has no speech and makes very little attempt to communicate. She is ambulant but wears splints to straighten her ankles. Sarah's class teacher reported that she responded well to rebound sessions, also to swimming, and music and movement. A copy of Sarah's educational objectives was made available by the class teacher and those which were relevant to rebound therapy sessions were noted.

Although work with Sarah for the purpose of this study began in November, her rebound sessions had begun six months earlier. During the first few weeks Sarah was helped to climb on to the trampoline and encouraged to crawl around the bed so that she could become used to the feel of the trampoline and the environment in which she would be working. Sarah then progressed through the following stages between May and November.

1. Sat in a cradle with two adults supporting and bouncing gently.

2. Adults moved back slightly to slowly reduce support.

3. One adult only kept Sarah's legs straight between adult's legs. No back support given to encourage Sarah to sit independently.

4. Stood with two adults, one behind holding hips and one in front holding Sarah's hands. Gentle bouncing.

5. Stood on bed with two adults but no support given. Sarah encouraged to walk between adults.

6. Hoop introduced. One adult in front and one adult behind. Sarah stood inside the hoop and held the hoop with both hands. Gentle bouncing.

7. Stood alone. Adults depressed the bed slightly. Sarah tried to jump alone. Adult offered hands for support.

Although this records the progression Sarah made from a motor development point of view, the observations which were subsequently made focused on the area of communication rather than on motor development.

Objects of reference are used with Sarah to help her to understand the structure of her day. Her object of reference for the rebound sessions is a wooden frame with rubber bands stretched across it in both directions to represent the bed of the trampoline. On the window sill in her classroom is a row of shoe boxes and at the beginning of each day Sarah's timetable is communicated to her by placing the object of reference for each activity in the shoe boxes in the correct sequential order. When it is time for a rebound session Sarah is taken to her calendar boxes and the adult working with her co-actively removes the object of reference and makes sure that Sarah recognises it by moving her hands over the surface a few times. On most occasions when Sarah was observed, she set off, without prompting, for the sports hall where the trampoline is situated, as soon as she felt the object of reference. Sarah takes the object of reference with her and puts it down once in the sports hall. When the rebound session has finished she is encouraged to carry the object of reference back to the classroom and replace it in the appropriate calendar box thus indicating that the activity has finished.

Whilst working with Sarah during these sessions I wore an object of reference myself to distinguish me from the adults who usually work with her. This was presented to Sarah each time I approached her. Her regular classroom assistant also used her own object of reference and therefore before a rebound session Sarah was presented with three objects of reference, one for the activity and one for each of the adults working with her.

A Total Communication approach is used with Sarah, therefore objects of reference are not the only method of communication used. The adults working with Sarah use Sign Supported English. This means that a sign is used with the spoken word to reinforce meaning. The two signs used with Sarah during the rebound sessions were MORE and FINISH. Once Sarah was on the bed and involved in an activity, e.g. bouncing in the hoop, the bounce would be stopped after a countdown of five and Sarah was encouraged to sign MORE or FINISH. The activity would then continue again for a short time or would stop. This sequence would be repeated several times for each activity and signing encouraged each time the activity stopped.

In addition to the weekly observations made on Sarah, two other groups of children were also observed. One was a group of three girls aged between four and five years, also with dual sensory impairment and additional severe learning difficulties. This group was observed on two occasions two weeks apart. Field notes and a video recording were made. Again the observations focused on the opportunities for communication both for the adults and the children. This group of children was at an earlier stage of development than Sarah and rather than conventional signs being used, the adults were looking for any signal from the child which indicated PLEASURE/DISPLEASURE, MORE/FINISH.

The second set of observations were made of a group of older children, ages ranging from thirteen to nineteen years. These children had severe learning difficulties in addition to dual sensory impairment. Two of them also had severe behaviour problems. Again field notes were made but it was felt inappropriate to make a video recording of this group in order not to disturb the normal routine of the session.

Analysis

The length of this chapter does not allow for an analysis of body image and spatial awareness, which are important elements of any rebound programme. The analysis will therefore concentrate on the following aspects of communication as identified by Ouvry (1987):

- pre-intentional/intentional

- receptive
  - tactile clues
  - visual clues
  - auditory clues.

- expressive
  - satisfaction of needs
  - control of the environment
  - regulation of personal interaction.

The examples of pre-intentional communication which were observed included smiling, laughing, facial expressions which indicated uncertainty, physically reaching for adult for reassurance, and so on. These behaviours could be interpreted as reflex responses, or pre-intentional communications in response to the external stimuli which were being presented to the child at the time.

It was apparent from the observations made that all the children had very quickly moved from the pre-intentional stage of communication to the intentional stage once they were on the trampoline. Without exception, each child was observed at some stage to communicate in a positive way that they wanted an activity to start or stop. This was demonstrated in a variety of ways which were different for each child. The following list shows the variety of ways to indicate MORE:

1. Moving legs up and down.

2. Banging trampoline bed with hand.

3. Vocalising.

4. Arching back.

5. Signing MORE.

6. Bringing hands back down onto bed after head banging.

7. Lying back down on bean bag on trampoline.

As most of the children obviously enjoyed rebound therapy there are fewer examples of ways in which FINISH or STOP was indicated by the children observed. The following list shows ways in which the children indicated that they wanted to FINISH:

1. Sitting down in the middle of the bed.

2. Sitting up from lying position.

3. Head banging.

4. Vocalising FINISH.

Both pre-intentional and intentional communication were observed while the children were taking part in rebound therapy sessions but it was very obvious that the trampoline was an ideal environment in which to give the children the opportunity to develop intentional communication skills.

Rebound therapy is an activity through which messages can be given to a child immediately. The child receives tactile clues through the movement of the trampoline itself and from the adults working with the child. Visual clues may be useful to children unless their visual impairment is such that these would be inappropriate. Visual clues can help children to orientate themselves on the trampoline as well as receiving instructions or questions from the adults. Auditory clues can also help children orientate, e.g. by having bells tied to the centre of the bed or beating a drum in time to the bounce. Adults can prepare the children for the next activity by giving verbal instructions.

Tactile clues were given to the children in a number of different ways depending on the needs of the individual child. Every child except one was given a physical prompt of some degree when getting on to the trampoline. This was because the trampoline was too high for the children to climb on independently even though crash mats were placed alongside in order to reduce the height the children had to climb. As well as providing the physical assistance the children needed to climb on to the trampoline it gave the adults working with the children the opportunity to have personal interaction with the children and therefore help them to identify who would be working with them.

Once on the bed a variety of tactile clues were given to the children. These ranged from giving the children enough physical support for them to be able to take part in the activity safely, to co-active signing with the children in order to communicate what would happen next. One child was given additional tactile information by a hoop being used to support her when she was bouncing. This took the direct adult contact away but gave her a substitute in order that she maintained her skill level. Another child, who tended to be tactile defensive and reluctant to accept human contact, was provided with a bean bag for support instead of direct adult interaction.

For children with visual impairment, visual clues may not prove particularly useful but in order to encourage the use of residual vision these cues should not be forgotten. Children with some degree of residual vision will receive visual clues as they enter the room where the trampoline is situated. They may be able to locate the trampoline and the adults who will be working with them. It is useful if the pads placed round the edge of the trampoline for safety are a contrasting colour to the bed of the trampoline. This will help the children to locate the working area. Children who were using signing as a method of communication were given visual clues by the adults in the form of signs. These gave the children instructions or told them what would happen next.

As with visual clues, auditory clues were used to a greater or lesser degree depending on the children's level of functional hearing. For some children the spoken voice was extremely important as they relied on receiving instructions and directions as to what would happen next. Others, however, were given clues as to where to locate the centre of the trampoline by listening to bells which were attached to the centre of the bed. Another method of clueing was by the use of a drum beat which was used to indicate to the children when to start and stop bouncing.

In addition to the children receiving clues from the environment and adults around them, rebound therapy also provides an excellent opportunity for the children to interact through expressive communication with those around them. Every child who was observed during this study exhibited some form of expressive communication.

Earlier in this chapter the needs of dual sensory impaired children were identified. During the course of my observations it became apparent that rebound therapy can satisfy these needs. These children need a reactive environment. The trampoline by its nature provides this. As soon as the children move onto the bed, the surface will react to the slightest movement made by the children. The trampoline provides a clearly defined environment so that the children experience security and familiarity whenever they are on the trampoline.

The movement routines through which the children progress provide structure to the sessions and the children are given opportunities to use their residual vision and hearing. By working with familiar adults in close physical contact the children are given the opportunity to build up personal relationships and learn to interact with those working with them. Most importantly, the children are given the opportunity to control their environment and the activity which is taking place through communicating at whatever level is appropriate for them.

As stated the environment of the trampoline provides opportunities for the children to control the activity which is taking place. It has already been stated that every child who was observed for the purposes of this study was able to control the activity to a greater or lesser degree. Each child had a method of communicating that they wanted more of the activity or that they wanted to stop. More able children can be given a choice of activity, e.g. 'Do you want to sit or stand?'

The advantage for staff working with the children on the trampoline is that the activity is immediately controllable which means that a quick response can be given to the children's communications. In this way the children very quickly learn that they can cause a change to take place.

It is important that children with a dual sensory impairment should not be tactile defensive since they rely heavily on adults in order to be able to interact with the world around them. Rebound therapy provides opportunities for children to develop relationships and to learn that they can have dialogue with the people working with them. Initially, it is necessary for the adults to have very close physical contact with the children for safety reasons. During this time the children are given the opportunity to develop trusting relationships with the adults working with them. As the children become more confident and the adults begin to move away the children learn that the dialogue still continues with the adults and that they can be in control of the activity by communicating with the adults.

During my observations it became apparent that the trampoline is an ideal environment for children with dual sensory impairment. It provides a confined identifiable area which they can understand. There is no clutter to confuse them and it gives them an opportunity to experience freedom and energy which they cannot find elsewhere. The results of this study have shown that rebound therapy can satisfy the needs which have been identified as being of paramount importance for dual sensory impaired children.

In 1966 Charles Buell wrote that 'trampolining can be great fun for visually handicapped children'. This surely is one of the most important considerations when working with dual sensory impaired children. So many activities in which they take part are not 'fun'. One of the over-riding impressions which was left with me as a result of this investigation was that the majority of children do find rebound therapy an enjoyable activity in which to take part. This must surely give added value if an enjoyable activity can also present opportunities for educational development.

The findings of this work confirmed that rebound therapy can provide a very positive environment in which to develop the communication skills of children with dual sensory impairments. The trampoline provides a restricted environment definable by texture and movement which reflects the idea of Lilli Nielsen's 'little room'. It is an area with which a child can become familiar and feel secure. It fulfils one of the requirements of McInnes and Treffry (1982), for a reactive environment. The child can learn to control this environment through signal behaviour which Visser (1988) considers to be the 'primary goal of communication'.

Rebound therapy also provides opportunities for co-active movement between adult and child which Wyman (1986) says is 'the basis for a great deal of the child's learning'. The activity is easy to control quickly in response to the signals given by the child and the child learns that s/he can be in control of the activity and make choices about what will happen next. It has been shown that, in terms of giving opportunities for communication, rebound therapy offers the criteria laid down by Mittler (1988) 'that the children want to communicate, that they have something to communicate about and that communication is enjoyable and brings results'.

Having established the benefits derived from using rebound therapy with dual sensory impaired children it would seem appropriate to discuss the implications for including this activity in the curriculum for these children. During visits to a variety of special schools in the North East, it became apparent that those members of staff who were running rebound sessions were very committed to the activity and were convinced of the benefits to the children. One school made a decision that on the afternoons rebound was to take place, the usual staffing ratio should be altered to give the rebound sessions priority because of the importance attached to those sessions.

Obviously, the main consideration is that a school has a trampoline. It is not necessary to have a full size trampoline, however, as the junior size is quite adequate, although it would not be appropriate to try rebound sessions on anything smaller. Having acquired the trampoline it needs to be located in a suitable room. This is often the school hall, gym, or sports hall. Wherever it is located, the position must be considered from the safety aspect. There must be adequate space both around the trampoline and above it. It goes without saying that suitable safety pads must be provided to cover the springs, and adequate crash mats placed around the edge of the trampoline. However, the children observed for this study were always accompanied on the trampoline with one, and in most cases two adults, so crash mats and spotters are often not necessary for immobile children. This must be left to the discretion of those running the sessions.

Having acquired and set up the equipment the next major consideration is that of staffing. Training must be the priority. Every member of staff taking rebound sessions should have the minimum qualifications of the Basic Rebound Therapy Course. These courses can be run by anyone with the Advanced Rebound Therapy Certificate. Neither of these courses is a substitute for a qualification from the British Trampolining Federation and they are not qualifications for teaching trampolining. In addition to appropriate training, Donsback (1980) and the DHSS (1986) have published articles on the medical aspects of rebound therapy which should be read by anyone planning to run rebound sessions.

Once the staff are trained the school must decide upon the commitment it will give in terms of time and staffing to rebound sessions. For the sessions to be of any benefit to children with dual sensory impairment the minimum requirement should be once a week. The more frequent the sessions the greater the benefit to the children. For those readers who do not have access to a trampoline, there are other movement methods, such as the Halliwick Swimming Method and the Sherborne Movement Method, which have been devised for children with physical, sensory and learning disabilities. These also provide similar opportunities for the children to feel the freedom of movement, have the opportunity to develop relationships, and to develop their communication skills.

Author's acknowledgement

I should like to acknowledge the contribution made by the children and staff of the special schools who allowed me to observe and take part in their rebound sessions. Without their co-operation this investigation could not have taken place.

References

Aalborgskolen (1991) *Deaf-blindness, one specific handicap.* Aalborg, Denmark: Aalborgskolen.

Anderson, E. (1987) 'Movement Education for Children with Severe Disabilities', *British Journal of Physical Education,* **18** (5).

Beachill, H. (1985) Rebound Therapy (unpublished thesis). Dept of Education, Sheffield City Polytechnic.

Buell, C. E. (1966) *P.E for Blind Children.* Springfield, Illinois: Charles and Thomas.

Coupe, J. and Goldbart, J. (1988) *Communication Before Speech.* London: Chapman and Hall.

Cratty, B. J. (1979) *Perceptual and Motor Development in Infants and Young Children.* Engelwood Cliffs: Prentice Hall.

DHSS (1986) 'Medical News – Neck Problems', in *Circular to General Practitioners and Schools, reprint from Down's Syndrome Association Newsletter.* Southampton: Hobbs.

Donsback, K. W. (1980) *What Do The Doctors Say About Rebound Excercise?* Edmonds WA: The National Institute of Reboundology and Health Inc.

McInnes, J. M. and Treffry, J. A. (1982; p'back ed. 1993) *Deafblind infants and children: A developmental guide.* London: University of Toronto Press.

Mittler, P. (1988) 'Forward', in Coupe, J. and Goldbart, J. *Communication*

Before Speech. London: Chapman and Hall.

Moody, M. G. (1986) The Introduction, Implementation, and Evaluation of a Programme of Rebound Therapy with a Group of Mentally Handicapped Adults (unpublished thesis). Bradford and Ilkley Community College.

Ouvry, C. (1987) *Educating children with Profound Handicaps.* Worcester: BIMH Publications.

Sherborne, V. (1979) 'The Significance of Early Movement Experiences in the Development of Severely Retarded Children', in Upton, G. (ed) *Physical and Creative Activities for the Mentally Handicapped.* Cambridge: Cambridge University Press.

Sherborne, V. (1990) *Developmental Movement for Children.* Cambridge: Cambridge University Press.

Stewart, D. (1990) *The Right To Movement.* London: Falmer Press.

Visser, T. (1988) 'Educational Programming for Deafblind Children – Some Important Topics', *Deafblind Education* **2** (1).

Williams, D. (1984) 'Rebound Education Therapy', in Brown, A., Brickell, D., Groves, L., McLeish, E., Morris, P. and Sugden, D. *Adapted Physical Activities.* Bodmin, Cornwall: Robert Hartnoll.

Wyman, R. (1986) *Multiply Handicapped Children.* London: Souvenir Press.

Young, J. (1986) Learning to Move – Educational Rebound Therapy, (unpublished thesis). Newcastle Upon Tyne Polytechnic.

CHAPTER 3

Objects of Reference

Marion McLarty

Objects of reference have been a component part of the methods in use for at least two decades to aid the development of understanding and communication in the education of dual sensory impaired children and young people.

The fact that the methodology has not been used more widely would seem to be due to the low incidence of dual sensory impairment and the fragmented and isolated nature of specialist educational provision. This situation has altered quite markedly in England and Wales over the past three years. GEST 29 (14) funding for the development of services for deafblind children and the Staff Development Courses which have been a major feature have led to an upsurge of interest in this previously very specialised methodology. Educational practitioners working with children with a range of difficulties (PMLD, communication disordered, etc.) have begun to realise that relevant use could be made of the methodology in their own sectors.

Four case studies

ALISON, aged fourteen, is profoundly hearing impaired and has a severe visual impairment due to maternal rubella. She is very interested in people and often attempts to involve them in what she enjoys doing most, looking at picture books and signing or finger spelling what she sees there. When she was very young doctors informed her mother that she would never read or write and that there was little hope of her achieving anything. This gloomy forecast has obviously been proved false.

Like many children with severe sensory impairments, Alison found life to be confusing and often frightening with little opportunity to have any control or choice in activities other than to withdraw completely. The use of the Dutch Conversational Method, with its emphasis on a strong relationship between adult and child, on a consistency of environment and approach and support for anticipation of events through the use of objects of reference, began to break down her fear and distrust and to make her a more equal participant in her own life.

Over a period of about ten years her use of objects of reference progressed to an understanding of symbols and development of skill in drawing and simple script. Along with this, natural gesture developed to become more commonly used signs so that today her main modes of communication involve BSL signing, a little finger spelling, her most favoured method being a combination of drawing and writing.

She is now at the age when parents and school staff are beginning to look to the future and it is hoped that a place will be found for her, at least part-time, in the special needs section of the college of further education nearest to her home.

CAROL, also aged fourteen, has a moderate to severe hearing impairment and has so little sight that she has used non-sighted methods throughout her school career. As a small child she presented as having little or no hearing and would refuse to wear her hearing aids, particularly in the left ear which tests now show to be stronger.

Carol's reaction to her difficulties was extremely dramatic and as a small child she spent a good deal of her time throwing tantrums. In fact this enormous energy and willpower probably served to keep her fighting the world when many of a less determined nature would simply have given up. Her lack of useful vision meant that she was able, initially, to make even less sense of the world than Alison. Her response was to kick, hit, bite, spit and even to punch herself until her nose bled. Again, as with Alison, the way to address her fears was to provide for consistency of staffing and activities, although her level of tolerance was so low in the early years that even a pause in brushing her hair was enough to precipitate a violent tantrum.

Eventually, however, life became less infuriating as it became possible to anticipate people and events. As she moved from full sized objects of reference to reduced and miniaturised versions and, very recently, to Braille, she began to regard the world as an interesting and enjoyable place rather than as a threat. She began to wear two hearing aids, she reacted to strangers with interest and curiosity and she smiled and laughed instead of screaming and crying. Very recently she made even more sense of the scrambled sounds which she had obviously been experiencing for most of her life and began to speak. At the present time her repertoire is confined to only a few words but her understanding and satisfaction are huge. She now understands that it is normal to say 'hello' and 'bye' and will respond with pleasure when greeted. No one can tell how much further this development will go but even now the change in quality of life for Carol and her family is far more than most of us would ever have imagined nine years ago.

The most interesting aspect of this particular case for me is that it demonstrates just how stressful the distortion of sight and hearing can be. Too often it is assumed that because a child makes little or no use of visual or auditory information then their sensory or learning disability is responsible for this. How often, we must ask ourselves, is it likely that the school and/or home environment are adding to the barriers to a child's learning through providing so much unusable and distressing stimuli that it is easier to blot this out and appear to be much more seriously disabled than they actually are.

PETER, who also suffers from the effects of maternal rubella, is a very bright alert nine year old with severe visual and hearing impairments. Placed originally in a nursery attached to a school for the deaf, he was reported to be a difficult child whose behaviour ranged from introverted to disruptive. His first few days in a school for deafblind children were a revelation to Peter and to his teacher.

Provided with a teacher who was there for him and with a structure which was both consistent and flexible he became at once more outgoing and less disruptive and energetically tackled any activities which were offered. Indeed, I have never, before or since, observed a child who wept at lunch time because it was interrupting his work.

As he did not enter the school for deafblind until he was six and a half, he had developed an awareness of the world which enabled him to understand the concept of symbols and so did not need to begin with objects of reference as such. He had, however, experienced years of frustration during which he felt unable to affect anything outside of his home environment and responded to this situation quite violently at times. He would often resort to kicking the attendant who accompanied him in the taxi to school and would behave anti-socially in the classroom to register his protest and feelings of helplessness.

It was necessary for him then to experience the security of a consistent routine where events could be anticipated and he would be assured that his efforts at communication were being understood. His programme began using pictures instead of objects of reference. The pictures were drawn by Peter, with a little help from his teacher, so that he was fully aware of the activity to which each referred.

The activities were those which would normally make up the

curriculum in a school for children with special educational needs such as dual sensory impairments, but Peter's control of events came from being enabled to choose the order in which he would undertake the activities. Each afternoon before leaving for home, he would arrange his timetable for the next morning so that he knew exactly what to expect. Any last minute changes to the routine (due to cancellation of swimming, horse-riding, etc.) could be fully discussed so that they were understood and at least tolerated. In this way Peter became a much more equal participant in his own education and the difficult behaviour, while not quite a thing of the past, at least became a much rarer occurrence.

CATHERINE, who is nine years old, spent a great deal of the first four years of her life in hospital and much of the time in intensive care, strapped to a bed and hooked up to drips and other life-saving but painful apparatus. This meant that her attitude to the world was one of apparent terror. She would scream when approached and touched, even by her mother, and wanted to spend her time lying on her back flapping her hands in front of her face.

Owing to her traumatic start to life and her regular long spells in hospital, Catherine reached the age of five, after two years on the school role, with very little structure to her life other than her attendance at school when she was well enough. In spite of highly trained staff employing methods tried and proven by van Dijk, no one seemed to be able to get over the hurdle of her determined rejection of everything and everyone around her.

At about the age of four and a half, however, her health took a turn for the better, her attendance improved and she began to form a bond with one member of staff. Gradually she would spend less time on her back screaming and would allow herself to be involved in activities. She began to show an awareness of surroundings, particularly for the route of the dining room, and she progressed to the use of calendar boxes.

At present she uses small calendar boxes with reduced objects (e.g. a teaspoon for lunch) obviously appreciating their symbolic nature. There is a general feeling that she is not ready to move to a more abstract system and, indeed, that it may never be appropriate for her. Instead, we have observed her to develop the level she is at to accommodate her own communication needs. She signifies her desire for a change in her programme by objecting to a particular object as she reaches it in the calendar box and reacts with pleasure when offered the opportunity to choose from another one.

She makes up her own signs for new activities which she has encountered informally and wishes to have included in her programme.

The security and structure which she has achieved through the use of this methodology have led her, like the other children described here, to regard the world as a fairly pleasant place which they can experience and appreciate with the help and support of understanding adults.

The methodology

As can be seen from these short descriptions, the one statement that can confidently be made about all children with sensory impairments of sight and hearing is that they are all individuals. None of the four children described experienced exactly the same difficulties or took identical routes in developing their own particular skills. There are, however, some similarities as well as differences amongst the four cases, the most striking being the need for an internalised structure with which to make sense of and impose order on their own lives.

How would we react if we had no control over our lives, if the day was made up of a fragmented stream of events which occurred, seemingly arbitrarily, at times convenient to other people and with so little structure or order that we were not even able to begin to anticipate what would happen next. If we think about this for a moment we will realise that this is often the case in schools for very disabled youngsters. The timetable may be on the wall, all the staff may know exactly what they are doing but for the most important people, the pupils, life *just happens* to them.

Let us think of this same situation in a slightly different context. It was known by secret police services in many parts of the world, and now by the general public, that a highly efficient method of obtaining information was to break a strong personality by removing structure from their lives. Only a few days of little and irregular sleep, meals served at unexpected intervals, and no control over events or even the ability to anticipate them, could cause a breakdown from which some never recovered.

An inner structure then would seem to be basic to our successful understanding of and communication with the rest of the world, and yet because of unstructured educational experiences or those whose structure is apparent only to staff we deny some of our most disabled youngsters the chance to begin to develop anticipation and memory.

A much more holistic approach to a child's experience in school with objects of reference providing aids for anticipation and memory can lead to a much happier and less frustrating experience for many children. However, in order to achieve this, care must be taken to ensure that real communication is being facilitated at every stage and that the objects of reference do not merely become 'window dressing' in our classrooms.

The problem for those wishing to make effective use of this method, however, is first to gain enough information as to the theoretical basis of the methodology and then to translate this into a meaningful approach in their own context. As objects of reference are concrete and obvious to the observer it is understandable that the process of using them should seem to be equally obvious and straightforward, but this is not the case. There must be some knowledge and understanding of the whole methodology in which the use of objects of reference is set as well as a constantly rigorous and reflective approach to their application if the whole exercise is not to become empty and meaningless.

The use of objects of reference is only part of a holistic approach devised by Dr Jan van Dijk and associated mainly with the unit for deaf-blind pupils which is part of the Institut voor Doven, Sint Michielsgestel, Eindhoven. Turiansky and Bove (1975) stress that this approach is 'not a method or a technique but a philosophy, a total way of looking at each child in combination with a flexible theoretical framework', and this in itself may cause difficulties for those working in establishments with different traditions and staffing levels.

It is, however, possible to make effective use of objects of reference without having all the resources to replicate exactly the Dutch methodology. What is necessary is an understanding of the basic components of the methodology so that these may be taken into account in the devising of our own approach.

Some attention to underlying theory, not only that of van Dijk but of Piaget, Vygotsky and Bruner, is also helpful if we are not merely to apply (and so run the risk of misapplying) an empty formula. David Wood (1988) states his belief that 'Children's knowledge... is often a product of the "joint construction" of understanding by the child and more expert members of his culture', and goes on to say that 'Bruner and the Soviet psychologists such as Vygotsky and his colleague, Luria, place far more emphasis than Piaget does on the role played by culture and its systems of symbols... in forming the child's intelligence'. Such systems have a dynamic, structuring effect on learning and development.

They are not to be viewed as the mere 'content' of thinking but seen as part of this structure and its activity. When the child learns a language, for example, he does not simply discover labels to describe and remember significant objects or features of his social and physical environment but ways of *construing* and *constructing* the world'. Wood goes on to quote Piaget's statement that 'Thought is internalised action'. This is an interesting area for study but perhaps more complex and time consuming than is useful for most busy classroom teachers so let me simply explain just why I find these statements so significant for those considering the use of objects of reference.

It is a common belief, shared by many who are familiar with a behaviourist approach to the teaching of communication, that labels (e.g. cup, spoon, etc.) can be taught in isolation and have been internalised when a child is able to repeat them independently, on request, a satisfactory number of times. What Wood reminds us of is that a spoon to a child is not just a label for a familiar object. It is what he eats his meal with. It may signify extreme pleasure if the child has a particular fondness for pudding and does not know whether to expect it or not. 'Spoon' is more than a name or an implement for that child, it is a means by which he can anticipate the type of meal. Similarly with Piaget's thoughts on action-in-the-world, the spoon as object of reference in the child's hand is more than a symbol, more than a label, is a component of the whole activity of eating and will remain part of the whole activity for the child for quite some before it is readily identified as a symbol for a meal.

It is relevant here also to consider some discussion by Vygotsky (1936 suppressed, 1956 re-issued, 1962 translated) on the processes a child experiences in learning speech. If we consider his argument, with regard not to speech but to symbols generally and objects of reference in particular, then it should provide us with some valuable food for thought.

> Wallan, Koffka, Delacroix and many others in their studies of normal children, and K Beuhler in his study of deaf-mute children, have found (1) that the discovery by the child of the tie between word and object does not immediately lead to a clear awareness of the symbolic relationship of sign and referent, characteristic of well developed thought; that the word for a long time appears to the child as an attribute or a property of the object rather than as a mere sign; that the child grasps the external structure object-word before he can grasp the internal sign-referent: and (2) that the discovery made by the child is not in reality a sudden one, the exact instant of which can be defined. A series of long and complicated 'molecular' changes leads up to that critical moment in speech development.

Those who are interested will find some suggestions for further reading at the end of this chapter but my main object in quoting these theories is to focus attention on the fact that there is not some special property in the objects of reference themselves but rather that we, the teachers, are employing them to 'fill in the gaps' in the process of communication development which our children experience and, in so doing, an appreciation of some theories of development of communication and language is useful.

Using objects of reference in the classroom

Relationships

This is a vital element in the child's experience of the world and one which is too often overlooked in our busy schools. Relationships are a central part of most people's lives and it is through a relationship with a known and trusted educator that children will be motivated to communicate. From the security and trust of a safe relationship we are enabled to reach out and cope with a wider and more demanding environment, but without the existence of that base the world is too threatening and it is easier to become introverted and reject everything as many of the most disabled children can be seen to have done.

It is useful sometimes to spend just a short time in reflecting on the school experience of children with dual impairments of both distance senses. Do they revel in the colour, the noise and the movement of the busy classroom or would they be more likely to agree with Sartre (1946) when he stated:

> So that's what Hell is. I'd never have believed it... Do you remember brimstone, the stake, the gridiron?... What a joke! No need of a gridiron... Hell it's other people.

The importance of a strong trusting relationship is reflected in the first two stages of van Dijk's methodology in what he calls nurturance and resonance. In practice, this means that the early stages of adult and child getting to know one another are as important as the later stages when the teacher can be more obviously seen to be 'doing something'. Often, in the desire to be seen to be working with a child, educators will launch into activities which make little sense to the child and may even serve to frustrate and alienate him.

It is important to identify one key member of staff to work with a child and to give that person sufficient time just to *be* with the child, getting to know his likes and dislikes, trying out various activities and taking careful note of the child's reactions. 'In the education of deaf-blind children, development or responsivity is only possible when enough hours can be spent with the child individually and undisturbed' (Visser, 1988). This activity will also be of importance in planning the first programme as it is advisable to concentrate on those activities which are actively enjoyed or at least tolerated by the child so that the programme will flow smoothly with no conflict over unpopular activities to interrupt anticipation and memory.

This key worker, along with other significant adults in the child's life, should be readily identifiable. There should be complete consistency as to where and how the child is met each day on entry to school and each member of staff should have some identifying feature which can be drawn to the child's attention to reinforce his knowledge. It may be something as simple as a large chunky necklace, a pair of earrings or a thick rubber band on the adult's wrist but all individuals should take care to have a feature specific to themselves in order to avoid confusion.

Structure

Of equal importance to a secure relationship is an environment which is structured so as to be readily understood and unthreatening. It is a generally accepted view amongst theorists in child development that children actively 'construct' their knowledge of the world and as this is so then it is the responsibility of those working with dual sensory impaired children to facilitate this process as far as possible. Just as we would not present a large steak to a six month old child and expect it to eat with gusto and digest with ease, so we must present an easily 'digestible' structure of the environment to the child whose communication system is not yet fully developed.

Before introducing the use of objects of reference we should be sure that their use will 'refer' to a routine which is ordered and simple enough for the child to 'digest'. A regular morning programme of about four or five activities occurring in the same place, same order and with the same person is a perfect basis for the use of objects of reference. Children should already be familiar with activities and find them enjoyable and undaunting if they are to be in the correct frame of mind to cooperate in association of object and activity.

Choice of objects

Once the child is settled into a simple routine then it is appropriate for the key worker to consider the most appropriate object of reference for each activity. Some of these will be so obvious as to require no thought at all (e.g. a spoon for mealtime), while others may require more consideration. It is important at this stage to remember Piaget's observation that 'Thought is internalised action' and to choose objects which are actually used during the activity. For this reason, also, while some objects of reference may be in fairly general use in the school it must not be taken for granted that each child will naturally use what others use. If the usual object in use for music/sound perception activities is a drum stick this will not be appropriate for the child who refuses to hold one to bang a drum but loves to beat a tambourine against different parts of her body. The meaningful object of reference for this child's music session is a tambourine.

It is important also that objects chosen should be meaningful for the child rather than for the adult. A toy bus might give us a clue that a bus journey is about to take place but be completely meaningless to a child with restricted knowledge of the world who is more likely to associate the clasp of his seat belt with a trip on the bus.

At this early stage there should be no attempt to over-emphasise the symbolic nature of the objects, rather they should be presented immediately before use so that there is no confusion as to their connection with the activity. This may cause difficulty in a classroom where, for example, the normal course of events is to prepare all children for lunch at 11.50 a.m. and then to spend a varying time singing songs until lunch arrives. If a child is presented with a spoon as an object of reference for the meal then the plate of food should be presented almost simultaneously with the spoon. An object of reference presented ten or fifteen minutes before an event will, at this early stage, either lose all significance or build frustration and anger when the expected event fails to occur.

Calendar boxes

Once children have been working within this secure programme with a known adult for some time they will begin to show signs of a growing awareness of the connection between object and activity: this may happen with some children after just a few weeks while for others this will take months or even years to develop. Perhaps they will smack their lips when handed the spoon or, if at a short distance from the table, make for their seat and sit down. It is possible for the teacher to test this out by beginning to distance the object of reference very slightly from the activity and watching closely for any signs of anticipation.

At this stage then, the concept of what van Dijk calls a 'day rhythm' is reinforced through the use of a calendar box. This may be made up of a number of small baskets or shoe boxes taped together. If a child has five activities and then lunch in his morning in school then there should be six compartments to the box.

In the first instance the objects should be arranged in the correct order by the teacher before the child arrives so that the child will simply feel the first object co-actively, make the sign/natural gesture for the activity (co-actively in the first instance but then progressing to independence), and then set off for the gym, music room, etc.

When the activity is finished, it has been my experience that the best approach is for the object to be taken back to the child's base by the adult. There are conflicting views on this with some educators recommending that the child return the object to the box and even close a lid to emphasise completion of the activity. I feel, however, that the object is the signal for an activity to start and an empty box signifies completion without returning to consideration of the object. When, and if, the child progresses to a more symbolic stage than the purely concrete there will be opportunities to signify the completion of activities more definitely.

As the child's familiarity with the calendar box grows then the child and adult can begin co-actively to arrange the objects in the correct order before the start of the programme. During this stage the conversation is likely to involve speech and sign/natural gesture (on the part of the adult) and sign or natural gesture (either co-active or independent) on the part of the child.

A typical session might then resemble this:

Adult: What's first? (accompanied by a sign)
Child: (No reaction)
Adult: What's first? (accompanied by a co-active gesture)

The drumstick would then be lifted co-actively from the store box and placed in the first calendar box. This would then continue until all objects were distributed correctly and the programme itself could begin with adult and child returning to the first box, identifying the activity and setting off.

Eventually, depending on the abilities of the child, the process will become more and more independent thereby demonstrating the child's grasp of the sequence of activities which make up the day and his understanding of the consistency of most of his days in school.

Moving on

It should never be forgotten that, while objects of reference may provide us with a valuable aid to communication, they should be regarded as a step on the road to use of a mass media of communication such as speech, sign, reading/writing, Braille, etc. Children should use objects of reference for as long as they need them but as their understanding develops so should their mode of communication.

Knowing when to move beyond the concrete object is as important as choosing the correct objects in the first place. If a practitioner is constantly attempting to devise 'objects' for abstract concepts (e.g. yes/no) then the question must be: 'Is this actually the most appropriate mode of communication for this child?'.

If children can select an object which means 'yes' then, except in rare circumstances, it is likely they will have the physical ability to nod, blink or sign manually. If both physical ability and understanding of the concept are present then the aim must be for the child to be able to communicate his wishes to the widest possible group. In this situation an adherence to an abstract concrete symbol would serve to restrict rather than enable communication. It is important for staff to guard against becoming so used to objects of reference that they continue their use when it is no longer appropriate.

The progression may be to drawing, and hence to the written word, or to miniaturised objects and hence to Braille, but it must be as carefully structured as the original introduction to the use of objects of reference. Each step should follow logically from the one before and be obvious to the *learner* as well as to the teacher.

It is obviously impossible, in the short space of a chapter, to cover all the issues surrounding this methodology. There is, however, one person on whom the success of any methodology depends – the rigorous reflective practitioner with the ability to regard theory and his own practice with the same critical attitude. Such persons will not jump on any bandwagon but will listen and read, observe and consider their pupils and finally choose a method which is appropriate to the needs and abilities of those individual children and young people. I would commend this reflective approach as the most effective for all teaching and most particularly for the use of objects of reference which contain no magic, but, used appropriately, provide a valuable aid to understanding and fulfilment for many children with sensory and communication problems.

References

Sartre, J. P. (1946) *Huis Clos*. Hamilton.

Turiansky, K. and Bove, M. (1975) 'Methods of Language Development – Van Dijk', in Fiociocello, C. (ed) *Language Development of Multihandicapped Children*. Dallas, Texas: South Central Regional Centre for Services for Deaf-Blind Children.

Visser, T. (1988) 'Educational programming for deaf-blind children: some important topics', *Deaf-Blind Education*, 2, 4–7.

Vygotsky, L. S. (1962) *Thought and Language*. MIT press.

Wood, D. (1988) *How children think and learn*. Oxford: Blackwell.

CHAPTER 4

Multi-Sensory Rooms and Dual Sensory Impairment: Use and Design

Richard Hirstwood

The multi-sensory room must feel like a relatively new concept to many people in education. It has many different names and guises such as Snoezelen, Space Room and White Tower. The rooms themselves are often designated rooms like an unused classroom, a large broom cupboard, a separate area in the corner of a classroom or even the school hall. The room has a variety of lighting and sound effects which are more often seen in theatre or discotheques than schools. Projectors playing moving images on a white wall, tall columns of colour-changing water, bubbles in the corner and soft music playing are just a few of the components which traditionally make up the multi-sensory room. The walls and floor may be padded to make the area safer and softer and the general atmosphere of the room is one of tranquillity and peace. Rooms can be used for a host of activities such as relaxation, stimulation, communication, interaction and many other functions, and as such are a potentially valuable resource for a dual sensory impaired child for whom these opportunities do not necessarily occur naturally.

It was Ad Verheul, a psychologist based at the De Hartenburg Institute in Holland, who brought developments in equipment and thinking together in a structured form at the Institute. He designed a series of rooms for a range of relaxation and leisure activities for profoundly learning disabled people It was whilst working in one of these environments that Ad Verheul started his observations of how people reacted to their environments, and he began working on making the rooms more sensorily stimulating in that he introduced smells, music, touch and taste in random sessions. Eventually spurred on by the reactions of the clients for whom he provided the activities, he experimented with creating relaxing and active environments and it was really here that the Snoezelen concept was born.

At the same time in Great Britain schools were using dark rooms for visual stimulation and basic cause and effect work. Boxes with tactile effects hanging down and projectors shining inside had been commonplace in some schools for many years. Thankfully they still are!! These schools were using the same equipment as De Hartenburg but in a different manner. Education at many levels was a high priority in these rooms (or areas). Teachers were using the rooms for activities ranging from basic visual and other perception skills to advanced communication techniques. To this day we still see even the more advanced multi-sensory rooms being used for educational activities or for Snoezelen but rarely both. These rooms can be multi-functional and should be appropriate to the child's needs not those of the staff. As the children and adults we work with differ in their abilities then the multi-sensory room should differ and should be flexible enough to meet the needs of the children and the goals of the staff.

However, like much of the technology presented to us, the multi-sensory room is often seen as a strange place which is used only by the school enthusiast, a little like the 'Dungeon Master'. The rooms are often likened to the computer: when the person who knows about it leaves, that's it, it's out of commission in a cupboard or used in a meaningless way. Robert Orr (1993) has observed that 'The sessions I have run and witnessed, seemed to depend on the feedback the client was getting from the worker present, and it was the skills and intuition of that worker which transformed the "glitzy", stimulating environment into a comprehensible chain of events'. Many people who read his article disagreed with what he said and interpreted it in a negative sense, but like it or not he is right. Any experience or learning situation has to be designed for the child or group of children in the multi-sensory room.

People have been heard to say 'The equipment does not work, it's no good!' If the room is used inappropriately it will not work and will be of no benefit to the staff as a tool or to the dual sensory impaired child as a source of enjoyment and discovery. Training in the use of rooms and technology in general is imperative, otherwise the area may be expected to achieve something it never will. The room and its equipment is only as good as the staff guiding the scenario. A comprehensive knowledge of the equipment is important. Many people have not yet asked the question 'What do I want it to do?' It is pointless having a room full of 'glitzy' gear if nobody really knows how to use it. Robert Orr (1993) in the same article observed that 'My other hunch is that people who can make use of these rooms, can achieve similar ends in other locations'. Again I have to agree. If people think that the multi-sensory room is the only sensory experience we can provide then they are very wrong. It is also wise not to be fooled by the cost of the equipment. Just because you have an expensive fibre optic sideglow it does not mean that the children will not prefer a pencil torch. The room should be seen as a place which provides a set of tools to use: it is an option which may be very appropriate for some children, but not for others.

The multi-sensory room also suffers badly from 'terminology'. When I was a mobile disc jockey in the seventies an Optikinetics Solar 250 was a projector, a bubble tube was a bubble tube. Now they are pieces of 'sensory equipment'. Surely calling it a projector is much more appropriate than calling it (and other effects) 'sensory equipment'. If you want to alienate half the staff, tell them you are going to the multi-sensory environment to work on cognitive skills with the sensory equipment, that should scare them a bit! 'Sensory equipment' sounds so formal and daunting for the staff who are going to operate it. It feels like it is going to be vastly more complex than it really is! One school I visited called the multi-sensory room the 'sunshine room', which was de-terminologising and less daunting to the staff and, most importantly, the children.

So why do some rooms prove to be positive educational environments. Clive Smith (1993) partly describes the feeling in a paper for the NCET about multi-sensory rooms:

> Some 25 years ago I went to see my first real rock concert. The group was then very new, 'Pink Floyd'. Afterwards I was left with two abiding impressions that long outlasted the music, The first was the lights and the sound, not the music but the sound. The centre piece of the stage behind the group was a circular white screen onto which was projected huge images. The images of every description continuously illuminated the wall dragging everyone's attention to the centre of the stage. Occasionally the images ceased and the whole rear wall of the auditorium was lit up with a huge projection of melting fluid, colours flowing over the wall, the band, their equipment and down to the audience at the front. Everyone searched the stage following the moving, changing globules of red, green and blue, watching larger masses of colours they slowly broke up. The music itself could be tangibly felt as the air vibrated, the steady beat of the bass and the drums created powerful rhythms. The use of music's power to affect emotions is as old as mankind but the sensory attack that was now launched on audiences was something totally new.

This particular experience took place long before people were even thinking about using sound and light equipment in the education of dual sensory impaired children. Today the multi-sensory room is working on the same principle. The effects used are not things we would see in everyday use, so they can create an impact or memorable experience. Equipment can create the kind of sound, sights, smells and experiences which can be motivating and thought-provoking for anybody, but for a child with combined impairments of sight and hearing who finds access to these experiences difficult if not impossible, the potential is tremendous. The room can be relaxing but also a place which can be used to encourage many types of interaction.

What is the multi-sensory room for?

The staff may find the room very relaxing, but it is very easy to go into the room and switch on all the equipment and say 'Look, he is relaxed!'. But is he? If children are not told about the environment first, to gain an understanding of where they are going, what will happen when they get there and what is required in the room, then the experience may be anything but stimulating and relaxing. It could be a little like going to the dentist: you haven't been for years, you don't know what's going to happen, you don't know what the specialised dental tools are for, and you dread to think what he is going to tell you. The best thing to do is sit there and let it happen. The multi-sensory room could be confusing, even frightening, and a very traumatic experience for many children or adults if it is used inappropriately. However, it is an area which when used correctly and appropriately can be an exiting adventure for a dual sensory impaired child as well as having many contributions to make to that child's educational development.

Relaxation

One of the most common uses for the multi-sensory room has to be relaxation. But there is a big difference between relaxation and withdrawal. Relaxation is a very valuable activity. When the room is set up in an imaginative way the area *may* be relaxing. But before an area can be relaxing the child's preferences in lighting, sound and other sensory experiences must be evaluated. Soft music and liquid wheels are often associated with relaxation and if they are suited to the individual they will create the ideal situation for peace and tranquillity. The multi-sensory room may be the only place where an individual child or small group of children can get away from the stresses of everyday school and home life. If we wish to relax we often have our own favourite place to relax and favourite stimulus to relax with. But remember there can be many other factors which will contribute to a relaxing experience. Relaxation is not just about doing nothing. Children can really benefit from the experience of touching a bubble tube and controlling the projector. Some dual sensory impaired children can really benefit from the multi-sensory environment; they find that the atmosphere will allow them to discover what it is like to be in a situation where there is no pressure to perform, knowing that there is somebody there with whom they are familiar and whom they trust to help and encourage. This may not be just a teacher but may be a friend. The multi-sensory room may be the only place where the child with challenging behaviour gets the individual attention children often yearn for! Different approaches will need to be tried to create a relaxing environment. The liquid wheel and 'new age' music tapes are not always the answer. Every child has different preferences.

Stimulation

Many people say the multi-sensory room is an area where dual sensory impaired children who experience so little positive natural stimulation can be stimulated: but what is stimulation? My own interpretation of stimulation is getting a child to use and begin to understand his senses. The most obvious use for the multi-sensory room in this area is visual stimulation. The effects in the room lend themselves very well to this. Again, care and an initial assessment will be very important when encouraging the use of vision. The equipment can be engineered to give contrast, colour and movement. The projector can be used to create large images for some and small images for others. The light can be played on to a wall, inside a box, on to the ceiling and backprojected through netting. This is purely visual stimulation but if you project on to an interesting surface rather than just the wall then touch can also be motivated.

However, the multi-sensory room is not just about visual stimulation. It is about setting and achieving objectives or goals for an individual's other senses. Stimulation is often seen as valuable on the road to gaining life skills. Sound is an area which can be engineered in the room. Like visual disabilities, hearing loss takes many forms and again initial and ongoing assessment is important. Music is not always the key. As Clive Smith (1993) points out, his memory of the Pink Floyd concert was not the music but the 'sound'. We will need to consider the type of hearing loss as some sounds may be uncomfortable. Sound effects may be used from a CD or tape, and with a little imagination we can set different levels of sound at different pitches. Using percussion and many classroom objects, sound can be explored. Moving sound around the room may also be useful. With the advent of exiting new equipment like Soundbeam, sound can be linked in to movement.

Smell and taste can be explored as well as touch, but if a child's predominant sense is touch, it may not be wise to trivialise the experience with meaningless stimulation. This may lead to the child misinterpreting or feeling the activity is insignificant. At any level the stimulation should be interesting, enjoyable and most importantly it should be leading to future possibilities.

Bernard Gummet (1989) points out that sensory stimulation is often a missed opportunity for interaction in which all concerned are likely to benefit. Pupils will benefit from being valued for who they are and not so much for what they might become as their behaviour is modified. The staff will benefit from being able to enjoy a rich exchange of human interaction with their pupils as they share the experience of sensory stimulation. The equipment is not always the best tool in the multi-sensory room and it should not be seen as wasted if it is not used in every scenario. Sometimes the room itself can be the tool: it may be the atmosphere which it can create which helps the interaction between the staff and the child.

Interaction

In the multi-sensory room interaction can mean many things. To most non-technical people it means the interaction of people. Not just two but maybe more. One thing often said of the rooms is that they are successful because of the close interaction between the child and teacher. Do not take this as a criticism. It does say something about staff to children ratios in classrooms, but if the multi-sensory room is one of the only places where this ratio can be achieved, then surely it is a good thing. The trust gained can be built up as the ongoing experience of the room and communication between the people using it are enjoyed.

Interacting with the equipment does not always have to be about switching switches to make things happen. Dual sensory impaired children may be allowed to discover new experiences if the room is set up in a safe and meaningful manner. Touching bubble tubes or watching and feeling an image projected on to a net may be something which can be achieved only in the multi-sensory room. This may not just be about the equipment, but about the accessibility of the stimulus. In the multi-sensory room we can present the effects to a dual sensory impaired child in a way which can be made safe to touch, see and hear. If a child has a severe visual disability the room may be the only place where the light can be presented in an appropriate way. Correct lighting levels, lack of other influences (such as other children or other distracting visual equipment) and a single visual preference may be just some of the influencing factors. However, if the room is set up or managed inappropriately then the experience may not be suited to the child. The exploration of the environment, where a child is encouraged to explore the walls and floor and see what happens, may be encouraged.

The interactive approach, where switches and responses are monitored as part of the individual programme plans, will lead the room to be an enhanced assessment and development based environment. As the name suggests, the purpose of an interactive switching environment is to enable a dual sensory impaired child to exercise control over his surroundings, developing choice, motor skills, motivation and movement. A favourite activity (the effect) can be induced or started by means of a switch (the cause). A simple example of this would be a touch switch connected to a projector via a switching system. But with new controllers and switches you can have one switch controlling many pieces of equipment and multiple switches to allow choice. A good example is an interactive bubble tube with red, blue, green and yellow switches. The child can choose the colour of the tube by choosing which colour switch to press, as well as controlling the bubble flow. The children are able to be rewarded by performing a skill, be it movement or sound, and their favourite effect or activity is initiated by their interaction with a switch. These switches can then be used to help the individual gain independence (life skills) outside the room. Turning on a TV or radio, opening a door, moving an electric wheelchair, using a communicator or computer are just some of the skills we may wish to develop in the future, no matter how distant that future may be.

The switches themselves may be push-, touch-, sound- and even air-controlled. There are a wide range of switches available which will suit most tastes. Each switch is then linked to an effect, i.e. a projector, sound source or other suitable piece of equipment. Through assessment we will need to determine the correct switch to operate the equipment. We should be careful that the reward remains a reward and not a tediously annoying activity. This may be likened to watching your favourite TV programme. If you have a switch on a timed mode and every ten seconds the TV switches off, how would you feel? I am sure the controller would soon be thrown away due to frustration (or challenging behaviour as it is sometimes labelled). Again the activity needs to be thought about before commencement.

Clive Smith (1993) points out that:

> In many establishments switch training had become almost a curriculum area in its own right. Special needs software became devoted to switch operation. Multi-sensory rooms were devoted to switch operation. Unfortunately it would appear that in many situations the switches have stayed attached to the computers in sensory

rooms and on electrically operated toys. Within the schools themselves the switch operation never seemed to acquire a functional use beyond an academic exercise. The continuum should have been straightforward. At the most simple level we are trying to provide a series of links for our students. If he/she presses the switch the bubble tube goes on. If he/she presses the switch a tape recorder works and music plays. Moving on eventually leads to switching on other equipment and eventually household equipment, lights, TVs and other simple equipment building up increased life skills. Within some establishments this final phase is never attempted. With appropriate switching the students should be able to participate in controlling the classroom environment, switching on the tape or CD when music is required in the classroom, powering up the whole computer system when they wish to use it without relying on an adult setting it up.

How long will the session last? Is the switched reward the only reward the child will get? Will the session be enjoyable or will it be a stressful and frustrating activity due to incorrect positioning of equipment (The teacher says I'm doing great, but what am I doing?); wrong type of switch (I can do it but the switch is inaccessible!); the session becoming tedious (Why do I have to keep showing you I can do this?). These can be just some reasons why a child may opt not to operate a switching system. Too many demands on anybody can become a tedious chore, rather than a rewarding experience. Planning is so important when using switching systems because when a switching system is used appropriately the rewards for both the teacher and child will be very worthwhile.

Communication

This is probably the most important factor in a dual sensory impaired child's development. Communication at different levels is essential. It requires a sender, a code and a receiver. Often the code is the most difficult to identify. The sender and the code may be there, but the receiver is not because the intended receiver is either engaged in another activity in the classroom or is not interpreting the code in the way the sender (child) wishes. The multi-sensory room can create the ideal situation for understanding and recognising many of the signals. The argument again about the room only working because of the interaction between people is then turned round to make the room a positive experience. We may be able to look more closely at children's gestures, body language and informal or pre-verbal communication attempts. Initiation, expression of preferences and cause and effect are all part of communication skills which may be more identifiable in the multi-sensory room. If children are in a situation where they are comfortable then an effort may be initiated to let you know how they are feeling. Showing a mood or 'challenging behaviour' is not the only reason why a child may choose to communicate. The expression of happiness is just as much a valid reason to want to contact. With imagination, the multi-sensory room can create many reasons for *wanting* to communicate. Of course communication in the room is not only at a Gesture level. We can work and enjoy the more advanced communication modes. The solar 250 projector wheels rotate. When an appropriate wheel is made for the child we can encourage anticipation, so moving on to sequencing skills. To do this, we may use a wheel with a visual image which a child enjoys and recognises (maybe slides of parents or familiar people). Or we may wish to use an ultra slow rotator which means that the wheel will rotate once every fifteen minutes. This may prove more successful than the usual half-revolution rotator normally used, which may be a little fast.

Although switching systems often fall under the heading of 'inter-action' they are also about communication. People can communicate their preferences through switches. Using 'Objects of Reference' (tactile clues) on switches may again aid dual sensory impaired children in understanding what they are controlling. Although this may be an advanced way to help a child to understand what is about to happen, more simple symbols could be used to let a child know where he is.

There are many more ideas which with time, imagination and planning can make the multi-sensory room a wonderful place to encourage one of our most essential but often hard to express needs, communication.

Assessment

The multi-sensory room can lend itself to assessment, using and adapting outlines like the *Affective communication assessment* and the *Pre-verbal Communication Schedule (PVCS)* manual. But assessments should be carried out before going into the room to establish the most likely preferences and the best way for the child to access the effects or stimuli. When in the room things may happen which you may not have seen before, especially when the child is experiencing the room for the first time. The experience is new and there are new surroundings and experiences to discover. People often comment that the first impressions are the most telling. As the dual sensory impaired child becomes experienced in the environment the ongoing assessment will be important if we are to discover what the next stages in development should be. Using the visual effects for visual assessment can really work. However, do be careful to notice what is motivating the child. A bubble tube, for instance, has many stimulating factors. The visual effect is just a part of the attraction and the sound may be the stimulus which is encouraging the child to turn towards it or to move his eyes in the direction of the tube.

Some imagination will be needed to blank out the unwanted effect. Avoid covering projectors to blank out the light appearing from the rear of the unit, as air is needed to cool the body. This applies to many other effects, so be careful and consult the supplier if in the slightest doubt. Techniques such as back-projection can be employed to help with this problem. Bubble tubes are available from one company which are called 'interactive', using switches with the tube so that the child or teacher can control the colours, stop the bubbles and turn off the light, which will make assessment much more controllable. The video camera can be an essential tool, as many things can be missed when an assessment is carried out by one or two people. Footage can be studied at a later date to establish any missed opportunities.

Assessment does not have to be carried out with equipment traditionally associated with the multi-sensory room. The room may just have the right mood and surroundings to effect an assessment using tools more often found outside the room. The multi-sensory room can be used by therapists and the assessments carried out in the room will be a valuable source of information for the other activities in school and home life.

Theme work

This is a traditional area of use that has relevance to dual sensory impaired children according to their level of impairments and their stage of development. However, for some children it may be of value and themes can be created using an existing multi-sensory room. The equipment evolved from the theatre world and the theatre is all about themes.

The room can be transformed from being the multi-sensory room to the space ship, submarine or other imaginative scenarios. A large scale theme day was organised at a discotheque in Lancaster. The discotheque is really a large multi-sensory room as most of the components are the same. More than fifty children and the same amount of staff attended a 'beach party'. The theme was to run for an hour and with the effort of teachers a story line was put together. The lighting technicians programmed robotic lighting to carry out the moves which would enhance the theme. Songs were sung and the lighting and sound effects were used to simulate the sun rising, the heat of the sun, the sound of the water, the surfers and the fairground at night. A theme does not have to be a full scale production. It can be a small scale idea in the corner of the room or even in a class-room aimed at one person. The theme can be a continuation of a theme which is being carried out throughout the school.

Will the room be the cause of seizures?

The National Society for Epilepsy (NSE) indicate that there is no evidence to suggest that flashing light *causes* the photosensitive trait to develop, merely that it can trigger seizures in people harbouring this trait. Photic seizures are subdivided into types, one of which is described as those who have clinical seizures triggered by a wide range of light or patterns of the intensity or type present in our environment (e.g. the domestic TV screen, sunlight coming through a line of trees, flashing lights and strongly patterned decorations).

This then indicates that a seizure could occur when exposed to flashing lights in a multi-sensory room. Flickering light at approximately 8-30Hz and certain strong geometric patterns are particularly powerful triggers of seizures (some subjects are also sensitive to frequencies outside this range). Environmental stimuli are enhanced by the closeness to the source material and its size, the configuration, contrast and luminance of the stimuli, and personal factors such as age, concentration or fixation on the material, emotional factors and fatigue. 8-30Hz is equivalent to 8 to 30 flashes per second. The frequency of flicker stimulation which is most likely to provoke seizures varies from person to person. In general this is between the frequencies of 5 to 30 flashes per second.

However, photosensitivity is rare and will mostly affect children around junior and secondary school age. There are other types of seizures provoked by problem solving, calculation, startle, music and reading. Emotional factors such as excitement and fatigue might be potential triggers for seizures. Only a small proportion of people with photic-induced seizures have a known family history.

It is likely therefore that the above factors are more likely to be enhancers in photosensitive individuals rather than acting on their own. Blanket restrictions should not be put on all children with epilepsy. The majority are not photosensitive and whenever possible they should be allowed to lead as normal a life as possible without further stigma, isolation or disadvantage.

Developing and designing a multi-sensory room

The **size** of the room is dependent on what you intend to do with it. Small rooms can work just as well as large rooms. If you want to work with groups of children then your room may need to be larger than a room for one-to-one work. The best room is around the size of a smaller classroom; this way you have the best of both worlds, and will be able to curtain off an area to make a small one-to-one working area. It is often best to have a separate room, but a darkened corner of a classroom would be a good start to a multi-sensory room. The room or area will need to be flexible as it may be put to many different uses.

The **colour** of the room is really up to you! Many rooms have been white, but now a move away from the pure white room has emerged. White reflects light and black will soak light in giving little reflection. You can project all round the room if it is white, which can be a great advantage in terms of accessibility of the projected image. In reality, projecting on to nets and sheets can make effects more accessible for most users, so white walls, floor and ceilings are less important. However, white will mean you can change the colours of the walls by using different coloured lighting.

Consideration should be given to the contrast of colour in a room. Not only do most of us find a totally white room very impersonal but it will give few clues to dual sensory impaired children about the size of the room, where the door is, etc.

When considering contrast remember that looking at a sideglow fibre optic against a white surface will show a diminished visual preference to that of a black surface. The same applies to many pieces of equipment. People are now finding that two colour rooms (black and white) can work well as they invite the flexibility of colour contrasts. There should be no reason why the room could not be in pastel colours, with coloured netting and sheets to offer contrasts. This way you will be able to vary the colour of the room to a child's needs.

Blackout is important to gain the best visual preference for a visual effect. If the room is dark then it will mean that the most prominent effect is the one you are using, not the sunlight shining through the curtains. The best way to black out the room is to velcro the blackout material to the window frame. You should always check the fire retardancy of the material you are using. Professional blackout curtains will also work very well but may be costly. If you decide to paint the windows that's fine but make sure you can still open the windows for ventilation.

Ventilation will make a room a comfortable place to work in. Not just on hot summer days but also on days when the equipment is in use for a long period of time. A friend in the air conditioning trade told me the air in a room should be changed at least six times per hour! Air conditioning is the best but the restrictions on most budgets will mean that extractor fans will be the most cost-effective option. Remember that the addition of soft floor and wall padding will insulate the heat. Noise is also a problem with a fan so it may need to be off if carrying out an assessment.

Room lighting (white) is still needed for moving people in and out of the room, cleaning and preparation of the next session. Most people do not like to be led into a dark room or a strange room with very few visual clues. Lighting on dimmers will be much more subtle and less stressful as you slowly take the room lighting up or down to an acceptable level. Although you will find this type of lighting more expensive, it can be a lot more flexible in its use.

The amount of **power sockets** will be determined by the equipment you require. The socket position should always be as close to the appliance as possible. If you have a solar 250 on a shelf at six feet, that's where the socket should be. Avoid trailing leads at all costs, and *do not* wherever possible use extension leads and adaptor plugs. When planning the room it is always better to have too many sockets than too few. The sockets should always have RCCD (or RCD) protection. This device will cut the power to a cable should it be severed or in the unlikely event of an appliance having a problem .

Furnishings will depend on the children's needs. Comfortable and correct positioning is very important. It will be difficult to enjoy and react to the stimulus if the child's main concern is pain or discomfort suffered due to bad positioning. Soft mats and wall padding can be used but allow access for a wheel chair and other mobility aids. A carpeted floor and the odd floor mat may be more practical to you than the floor and walls totally covered in soft foam. A room's ambience can be changed by having a multi-coloured floor using coloured mats. Wedges and rolls can function as good furnishings for support and access to the visual and sound effects in the room, and what about chairs?

Once the multi-sensory company leaves, having fitted the mats and the electrical equipment, the room can look very desolate and bleak especially if it is white or very lightly coloured. The room now needs **humanising**, making it into a nice place to be and, most importantly, enter. If someone is led into a plain white room, it may feel a little daunting as children and staff are not used to rooms like this. Try not to create a stressful experience by introducing somebody into a threatening or alien environment.

Equipment traditionally associated with the multi-sensory room is not always the best solution for dual sensory impaired children. Why not use the lullaby lite show, pencil torches, foot spas, vibro massage tubes and all the other equally stimulating toys and tools the children may love, and the staff understand. There are just as many miracles created with a piece of reflective paper as with a sound light wall. As many Snoezelen authors will stress, the environment may be the key. Without wishing to trivialise the multi-sensory room it is just a room! You do not have to use the technical sound, lighting and tactile equipment to get the best from a situation.

In equipment positioning **safety** is a key factor. Equipment such as projectors, fibre optic light sources and others too numerous to mention can, even if fan cooled, still get hot. Most appliances are low voltage but will still require a 240v mains source. They should be well out of reach from the hands of children who, in their best interest, should not be allowed to touch them. But the problem is, then, if a projector is very high and immovable the staff will not be able to access the unit to adjust its position and change the effects. The inconvenience will mean that people will go into the room and experience the same effects in the same positions time after time. Then the room will over a period of time become uninteresting and not serve the staff or children's need due to lack of flexibility. More time is needed in the planning of the room to identify ways of keeping the room's flexibility with safety. A suggestion is moving shelving. Some people have used TV shelves but by far the best option for projection is a shelf which will move up and down (unicol), so it may be out of reach when necessary. Fibre optic light sources exist which can be taken from the wall and used on the floor safely, when access is needed. Try to keep the equipment as flexible as possible and do not limit its use by its position.

Overview

The multi-sensory room is an exciting and to some a new tool. It has tremendous possibilities but if used incorrectly can very quickly become an area which at best is stale and devoid of ideas and at worst may upset and confuse children with dual sensory impairments.

The multi-sensory room should not take over from more traditional educational activities, but can be used to complement the skills and programmes of both the child and the teacher. It will expand experiences and can play a major role in gaining essential life skills. The key to the successful use of the rooms lies in the teachers being given both time and training to develop a full understanding of the technology and the equipment potential to ensure fully appropriate use of the room, and not using the rooms for their own sake.

Make the most of these wonderful environments. They have not only given us some of the most imaginative scenarios ever offered to children but have also stimulated the minds and gained the involvement of many professionals.

References

Gummet, B. (1989) 'The uses of Multi Sensory Stimulation in the education of pupils with severe learning difficulties' (unpublished M.A. dissertation). Lancaster University.

60

NCET (1993) *An Introduction to the Multi Sensory Environment.* Coventry: NCET.

Orr, R. (1993) 'Life beyond the room?' *Eye Contact* **6**, 25–26.

Smith, C. (1993) 'The multi-sensory environment' (unpublished paper for NCET).

CHAPTER 5

The Educational Benefits of Reflexology for Children with Dual Sensory Impairments

Sylvia Povey and David Etheridge

Reflexology is a therapy with a long and honourable history. It is understood to have been used by the Chinese, Indians, Incas and American Indian tribes such as the Hopi and Cherokees of North Carolina. The Ancient Egyptians also practised this art, the oldest known artefact depicting reflexology being a wall painting which was found in Egypt in the Tomb of the Physicians, dated to 2330BC. The therapy as we know it today is mainly the result of the work of William Fitzgerald and his colleague Edwin Bowers, their combined work on zone therapy having been published in 1917. However, it was another American, Eunice Ingham (1879–1974), who singled out the reflex zones of the feet. After much research and dedicated work she charted out on the feet a 'map' of the body. The person who brought reflexology to England in 1966 was Doreen Baily a former student of Eunice Ingham. Today reflexology is used widely and in Denmark it is recognised as a valuable therapy within the Danish equivalent of the British National Health Service. The Russians too are finding that reflexology can complement traditional medicine and, with scientific testing, are pursuing the study from the physiological and psychological point of view.

Reflexology is based on the premise that constant energy flows through ten channels or pathways, referred to as zones, linking all organs, glands and structures in the body: in Eastern cultures this is known as 'chi' or 'prana'. These organs and structures are reflected on the feet and hand in miniature like a mini-map of the body. By a special therapeutic massage of the reflected areas the body is helped to maintain a state of balance. Reflexology is commonly used to soothe and relax but it can also provide the opposite effect in stimulating the body. It is excellent for the circulation and eliminating waste products. Reflexology helps with many common conditions such as migraine, depression, back aches, menstrual disorders and oedema as well as the many conditions resulting from stress. Common conditions amongst children that are often treatable through reflexology are bed wetting, asthma, constipation, ear infections, and colds. In some instances, 'surprisingly positive results have been achieved by massaging the eye and ear reflexes (blindness, deafness, ear infections)' (Goosmann-Legger, 1988).

Unfortunately, comparatively little work has been undertaken in relation to the needs of children, and even less in relation to children with special educational needs, although the work that has occurred has indicated a very rich field indeed. Laura Norman (1988) suggested that when working with babies, 'gently working the baby's foot provides pleasure and nurtures the bond between parent and child'. This bonding and development of emotional relationships continues as children get older and their hands and arms become strong enough to return the favour and apply reflexology on their parents' feet or hands. Reflexology can become an important part of the ritual of relaxation that is so vital to the bonding process. Indeed, Norman has suggested that reflexology is particularly acceptable to younger children since they like to give and receive and have not built up the many blocks and defences about their bodies that are common amongst older children. Young children are not self conscious, enjoying being touched in playful ways, and reflexology gives them a sense of security and nurturing. Indeed, reflexology sessions are particularly valuable for children who for a variety of reasons are not touched enough in their lives by family members. Hyperactive children have been found to calm down with reflexology and sluggish children are stimulated and energised. As suggested above, communication is enhanced and extended by the touching of the feet for, as Norman has observed (1988): 'As with adults, reflexology with children opens up pathways of communication between doer and receiver'.

Laura Norman did not work specifically with dual sensory impaired children, although early in her career she worked for a time with emotionally disturbed and multiply handicapped children. However, the little work that she did undertake suggested that these children became calmer, happier, more alert and able to learn faster. For children who have difficulties in forming close relationships with others, and who find the world of close sensory experiences incomprehensible, threatening, lacking in stimulation and enjoyment, and who find conventional communication difficult, the potential would appear to be considerable.

Reflexology application

Reflexology on an adult would average forty five minutes. However, for children the sequence has to be cut down to five to fifteen minutes, depending on circumstances. The movement used is like that of a worm or 'caterpillar' crawling. It should also be noted that the pressure when working with a child should be like stroking. The finger should be used if pressure is too heavy with the thumb. Figure 5.1 gives the sequence of reflex areas on the foot:

Figure 5.1 Sequence of reflex areas on the foot

DIAPHRAGM/SOLAR PLEXUS
Underneath ball of foot

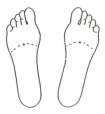

HEAD
Big toe, back and front
and
PITUITARY
Middle of big toe

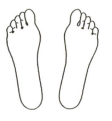

MASTOID PROCESS

EYES AND EARS
Beneath small toes

64

Figure 5.1 cont'd.

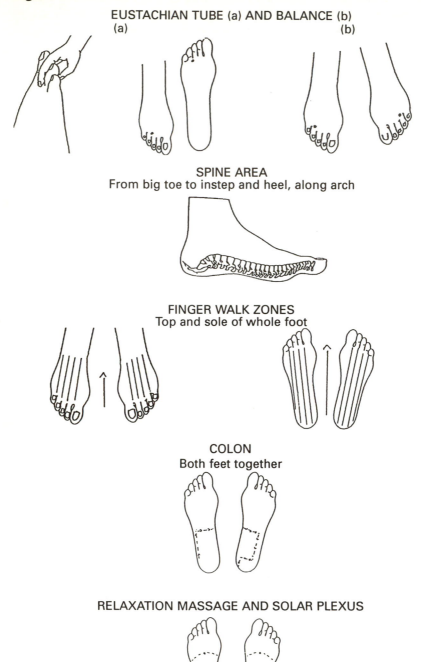

EUSTACHIAN TUBE (a) AND BALANCE (b)

(a)   (b)

SPINE AREA
From big toe to instep and heel, along arch

FINGER WALK ZONES
Top and sole of whole foot

COLON
Both feet together

RELAXATION MASSAGE AND SOLAR PLEXUS

Touch necessarily plays a very important part in the world of a child who cannot gain accurate information about his environment from the two distance senses of sight and hearing. Flo Longhorn (1992) suggested that touch for a multi-sensory impaired child:

- conveys unspoken words

- stimulates

- relaxes

- warns of danger

- demonstrates affection

- relaxes the body

- relaxes the mind

- polarises energy

- bonds people together

- provides identification.

Indeed, touch is a vital sense in helping to gain information about the world and developing knowledge of self for a child whose impaired sight and hearing often confuses and frightens. However, as McInnes and Treffry (1982) have observed, until the child has learned:

> ... to accept input from one sensory modality, too much stimulation can be as detrimental as too little and may cause him to 'turn off' and function at a lower level. The child must receive only the amount of sensory input which he is able to tolerate, interpret, and integrate.

The inability to integrate the sensory input from the various systems into a meaningful whole may cause that child to ignore inputs from several if not all systems.

Reflexology combines the benefits of massage and touch with the additional advantages that therapy can bring. By concentrating sensory stimulation in one area it can therefore provide a gradual, controllable and localised form of sensory input that will inform the child and give him access to a range of sensory experiences that can supplement and enhance a broader programme. The feet are not only a particularly receptive area of the body but, through the therapeutic form of massage that reflexology brings, can enhance and extend foot massage. Through direct stimulation of reflex areas on the feet, other parts of the body can be stimulated and a better state of homeostasis (balance) achieved. Feet are also removed from more immediate and personal parts of the body and do not pose the threat to self that other forms of touch and stimulation do. Indeed, it is useful to note that working with the feet in any educational programme with children has an added advantage of not using massage on the trunk or other areas of the body that might be lead to misunderstanding of abuse.

There are also additional benefits that reflexology can bring to foot massage. It does not use essential oils and therefore there is no need to remove the child from the classroom situation in case the vaporisation of the oils into the air has an adverse effect on other children. It can easily be used in schools with little disruption to the environment of the classroom or to other everyday activities. This is particularly important for most special schools, which are likely to have one or two dual sensory impaired children integrated into a larger group of children with other learning difficulties.

Foot massage through reflexology can therefore have many benefits for a child with a dual sensory impairment of sight and hearing. It can:

- help with desensitisation as a first step to develop tactile tolerance

- help with the development of body awareness, awareness of limbs and body movement

- encourage anticipation

- increase tolerance of new movement experiences

- provide a range of sensory experiences not available or acceptable through other methods of touch or sensory stimuli

- provide the child with a range of occasions for communicating pleasure, pain, anticipation

- improve sleeping patterns

- provide opportunities for the building and development of relationships

and, most importantly,

- provide opportunities for fun and enjoyment.

Longhorn (1992) has suggested that of the many resources important for the educational development of dual sensory impaired children 'the *most important* resource in this area is *human contact*', and of all sources of human contact for any child the most vital is that of the family. Laura Norman (1988) stressed the contribution of reflexology for the families of children with special needs:

Raising a chronically ill or disabled child can require heroic commitment from every member of the family. Family life will not be normal. Parents are sure to suffer disappointment and may even feel guilt, thinking that somehow they are to blame; other children may grow resentful of the ill child who demands more attention or puts a damper on family activities. Loving and caring for a disabled child can generate enormous amounts of stress. Reflexology can come to the rescue, especially for the ill or disabled child. It can alleviate boredom, improve circulation, and even become a kind of social activity if you teach the child's friends to do reflexology. Visits from peers can be more than just chitchat and games of gin rummy. The children can visit with a higher purpose of being part of the health care team.

Indeed, Norman (1988) emphasises the ways in which the family can be brought closer together to the benefit of all.

On many levels the family with a disabled child needs relief and relaxation, time for meditation and reflection. Reflexology is not a panacea, but it can provide the quiet time of being together, releasing physical tension in the body, and renewing your commitment to providing the best family life you can. Fear often accompanies illness, especially lingering illnesses.

Reflexology can act as a gentle reassurance that everything will be all right. It can alleviate parents' fears also because having reflexology at their disposal lessens their feeling of powerlessness in dealing with their child's illness.

However, a warning should be mentioned at this point. The practice of reflexology can effect physiological change and therefore must take into account the physical well-being of the client. It is vital that a practitioner is aware of the reactions that reflexology can effect and should therefore be undertaken either by a qualified practitioner or under the guidance of a qualified practitioner. As Renee Tanner (1990), has stated:

All reflexologists whether working for family and friends or as professional therapists need to have a basic knowledge of anatomy and physiology. The professional therapist needs to have a very good working knowledge of the body's structures and functions... I would always advise that if you are treating others in a professional capacity you undertake a full course of training.

Teachers, parents and others using reflexology must be trained if the benefits to dual sensory impaired children are to be realised.

The work that gave rise to this study was carried out in three schools for children with severe learning difficulties. It lasted for a period of six months and was attached to the Regional Advisory and Assessment Centre in Newcastle Upon Tyne. Although the work has only just begun and this chapter can only suggest areas for development, it is being undertaken by an increasing number of parents, teachers and other professionals in the region who are directly involved in the daily education of dual sensory impaired children. Cameos of some of the children and the benefits that they obtained from the application of reflexology are included at the end of this study.

Each of the establishments in the study had different needs and therefore approached reflexology in different ways. Indeed, it is important that reflexology, if it is truly to benefit the child, should be part of a holistic educational approach which incorporates it into the child's educational programme and also becomes part of the team approach which is so important for dual sensory impaired children. In one of the schools the most appropriate application was to work with the physiotherapists to incorporate reflexology into the children's physio-therapy programmes. The group of nine children (two of whom had dual impairments of both distance senses) that was identified was an all-age group who met together once each week for a specific physiotherapy programme. After putting into practice a small amount of work herself and listening to feedback from the professionals in the schools the physio-therapist decided to set up her own study programme. Specialist advice was still provided on a consultancy basis. A second physiotherapist did the same in a nursery.

The parents were brought into this as part of their usual involvement in this Movement Programme. It was felt to be particularly important that parents should be involved in order to provide greater continuity in programmes and also to allow those parents to develop benefits involved in the building of relationships and communication with their children. Reflexology was identified by these parents as being of particular use at bedtime, and when regularly used it not only provided a source of pleasure and fun but also appeared to improve the children's sleeping patterns. This may have been the result of greater relaxation at bedtime with nightly massage and reflexology on only the diaphragm and solar plexus reflexes: it is important that a full reflexology session should be used only once or perhaps twice a week since it may over-stimulate the child and compound sleeping difficulties. However, it is also possible that the therapeutic effects of relaxing both child and parents through this massage creates the natural separation that Dilys Daws and others have suggested is necessary for the child to fall asleep and also to sleep through the night without waking (Daws, 1989). Whatever the reasons for improved sleeping patterns reflexology does appear to have a very real contribution to make to one of the many and exhausting challenges faced by parents of children with sensory impairments.

In a second school it was felt that a more structured and integrated approach should be used in order to make reflexology a major part of the daily curriculum for a class of five children with profound and multiple learning difficulties, four of whom also had impairments of both distance senses. During the first five consecutive weeks' work of one morning a week, the main emphasis was placed on using a full reflexology treatment of 5-15 minutes with emphasis given to the eye, ear and spine areas; to get to know the children and build up the relationships that would be needed to work effectively with those children. It was also useful in that it allowed for the monitoring of the work, making sure that the children did not object to the application and that there were no adverse reactions.

After five weeks a team was formed with a specialist Advisory Teacher for deaf-blind children and the class teacher. The team felt that reflexology had very specific benefits for each child and that, most importantly, if it were to be effective it would have to be built into the children's educational programmes. A morning programme was jointly devised in which reflexology contributed to sensory/touch activities. The work was undertaken alongside the two class teachers and the two nursery nurses attached to the class, all four having been taught the reflexology routine

The morning consisted of three activities. For each activity the same adult worked with the same child. A set routine was established which took place in specific areas of the school. In this way consistencies of person, event, place and time were established. After the usual introductory start to the morning the first activity of the day was a co-active movement routine devised for each child and carried out individually with co-active signing. This was followed by a break for a drink. Reflexology became the second of three activities. Again the activity was introduced by a co-active sign, this time for 'playing with the feet'. A game was made of cleansing the child's feet with water, cotton wool and a pleasantly smelling liquid soap. These provided tactile and sensory clues along with the towel for drying the feet: this could be varied with surgical spirit, witch hazel, or tonic for cleansing. During the commencement of the massage which always precedes a reflexology routine everyone sang the 'Foot song'. After the massage the reflexology routine commenced with the 'Wiggly Worm' song, particularly appropriate because the movement used to apply reflexology is the finger creeping along the skin like a worm or caterpillar walking! The children's socks and shoes were replaced and the co-active sign made for 'finished'. The third activity consisted of further sensory stimulation based firstly on the hand, then on taste and smell. The hand stimulation consisted of massage to the palms and fingers with the 'jiggle song'. Tasting and smelling of a variety of different items for stimulation followed. The activity 'finished' in the normal way. As for the benefits of the sessions, one of the teachers involved summed these up as: 'aid to movement; aid to understanding; body awareness; increased toleration of handling; evoking a response; showing likes and dislikes; recognition that touch has meaning, e.g. towel stroke as a reward; development of relationships including co-operation; enjoyment; preventing deterioration of the physical state; and communication'.

The morning provided activities which met general aims and specific objectives within each child's educational development programme. For school purposes the whole programme was formalised in writing for each child's record. A record sheet for the activities provided an opportunity to observe and comment on the programme for each session. The staff even made a bordered poster of the reflexology routine. As the headteacher of the school suggested, the programme was absolutely beneficial 'not only for the children but for the staff and the collaborative nature of the work'. Of particular importance was evaluation through discussion and videoing for school records. She identified the importance of reflexology being taught professionally rather than on an *ad hoc* basis. Indeed, the programme has been embedded into the larger educational programme for the pupils and has been perceived as 'a natural marrying with other aspects of education'.

Work in the third school involved two all age classes of children with severe and multiple learning difficulties from which two children had been identified as having dual sensory impairment. One particular class was working towards Key Stage 1 of the National Curriculum. Reflexology was used to supplement and enhance this programme promoting relaxation, invigorating and improving bodily functions and general health. The class teacher identified the benefits of reflexology to her, using it:

> ...to develop bonding, communication, body image and awareness in space. In building up a bond communication skills can be utilised. The speaking and listening involved in the Reflexology routine is incorporated within English Attainment Target 1, whilst using signs and clues incorporated into a programme meets the requirements for English Attainment Target 2 Reading, and body awareness and positioning can be used in Mathematics Attainment Target 4. In

Science Attainment Target 2 – Process of Life – the children are presented with opportunities to learn about their own bodies which promotes their five senses and experience of reflexology in the multi-sensory room on the vibrator board allows the children greater opportunities to develop these skills.

Changes within the National Curriculum are currently under review and it may therefore be necessary to adopt and review targets looking at how reflexology is incorporated into the curriculum. The class teacher went on to emphasise how important it is for teachers to have appropriate training because of accountability. She also felt that professionals within education authorities need to extend their awareness and realise the benefits within education.

There appears to be considerable potential benefit from reflexology for dual sensory impaired children. It gives the children another opportunity to improve well being and their quality of life. For children with so many complex problems we cannot afford to dismiss anything which may be useful and we should try it as long as it is not going to be detrimental to the child and as long as it works for them.

What is important is that the work started in this study should go on, with the proviso that it should be carried out by people who are trained and will not put the child at risk. All schools involved in the work stressed the importance of this, one teacher suggesting that advice and guidance might be provided using the model of 'a peripatetic music teacher until staff are confident'. There is a place for trained professional reflexologists, with an understanding of dual sensory impaired children to work with other professionals involved in their curriculum. The problem here, however, is a very practical one of finance and availability. Alternatively, teachers, nursery nurses or physiotherapists working within the schools could undergo a course of professional training but this necessarily means competing with other important skills when prioritising staff development programmes. The indication from this work in three schools is that they are willing to make this investment.

Cameos

1. Craig

Craig is four years and ten months old with cerebral palsy and impairments of both sight and hearing. His mother was bothered about the fact that he kept biting himself when demands were made of him outside his safe environment. Craig's eczema was also a constant source of irritation for him. He rarely gave eye contact, showed interest in people or expressed positive satisfaction through smiling or other methods of communication.

It was obvious from the first reflexology session that it was something that Craig enjoyed and throughout the majority of sessions he smiled and 'snuggled' further into the bean bag on which he lay. He also put out his tongue and vocalised with his 'raspberry' sound. A 'Foot Song' was used to introduce each session. A relationship was gradually built up over six weeks through reflexology sessions. Despite his lack of eye contact and apparent indifference no negative reactions occurred and Craig began at last to smile as soon as he was laid on the bean bag in anticipation of his feet being touched. One week after leaving him on the bean bag to rest the nursery nurse observed him drawing up his leg and touching his own foot. Occasional eye contact also began to appear, with sideways looks pretending not to watch what was happening during the sessions yet, in spite of this apparent indifference, watching and being aware of what was going on.

Craig also began to maintain body contact. Moving from the right foot to work on the left he sought a forearm with his free foot and let it remain there during the session. His vocalisations also developed a giggle. Craig found the sessions calming and massaging his feet soon became a way of reducing his frustration and producing a smile. Indeed, he began to show signs of anticipation, reaching out on arrival.

A programme for Craig gradually emerged from the early introductory sessions. After the initial introductions and a five to ten minute reflexology session Craig was put in the reclining position of his tumbleform chair with his feet placed on a 'pat mat'. Firstly his feet were moved co-actively up and down on this and he was then left to do it himself – which he would do when he chose. Afterwards he was given the 'baby gym' with a variety of objects both of a tactile and auditory nature.

On the health side, relaxation has certainly been provided as his hands and arms visibly relax during reflexology. His mum also stated that he does not bite himself so much and his eczema has also improved, although it has not completely disappeared.

2. Brian

Brian is a three-and-a-half year old child with impairments of both distance senses and cerebral palsy. The amount of his residual vision is not known but he does appear to track moving lights. His breathing is constantly laboured and relaxation is not easy. He likes being held by his mum and seems to relax more with this security. Brian has a part time placement at a school for children with severe learning difficulties. The school has a vibrating bed in their light room and Brian likes to relax in there on the bed.

On meeting with his teacher it was decided that during the weekly visits she would first of all give him some physiotherapy exercises, after which he would go on the vibrating bed and this would be followed by reflexology. The body contact would be advantageous for working on body image, self awareness and body contact.

It was clear from the outset that Brian enjoyed the reflexology because of his smiles and vocalisation and his hands would relax. He would also still from his uncontrolled kicking. A strong relationship soon seemed to build up and Brian showed recognition with smiles and vocalising when in close proximity. As the weeks progressed Brian's kicking also began to be animated in anticipation. He sought out body contact with his free leg during the sessions. Brian also began to initiate contact through reflexology. On completing the reflexology his feet would be held whilst talking to his mother. Brian would then shuffle his feet. Indeed, he also began to search for the hands with his feet.

Brian's mum learned the reflexology routine and she applies a full programme once each week and massage before he goes to bed each night, treating the diaphragm and solar plexus reflex areas. She has noted quite dramatic improvements in his sleeping patterns. He would wake up in the night and again very early in the morning. Brian now regularly sleeps through the night.

Brian's teacher has observed a real change over the last six months and she is probably the best person to describe his progress:

> Prior to this programme being established Brian was often distressed when handled and positioned, his sleep patterns were erratic and he was regularly constipated. Throughout the duration of the programme there has been increased evidence of good responses to the treatments. Brian is responding favourably to touch and handling and he is generally a happier, more aware child. His sleep patterns have improved and he is less constipated.

Many people are sceptical about the uses of reflexology in special schools but obviously it is not used in isolation. It is used to enhance a child's learning capability by stimulating or relaxing via the body's energy channels. There is certainly clear evidence of Brian making developmental progress. He is establishing bond relationships and he has been known to communicate the wish for more contact from the adults involved by shuffle searching of his feet when contact has been withdrawn. Reflexology is seen by staff within our class as beneficial for all children – it is another means of developing communication and bonding, forming routines and introducing more structure into the child's day and improving bodily functions/ physiological effects.

Author's note

The study took place within a secondment from The Pensions Directorate Newcastle Upon Tyne to the Regional Advisory and Assessment Centre of Sensory Impairment North East.

References

Daws, D. (1989) *Through the night: helping parents and sleepless infants.* London: Free Association Books.

Goosman-Legger, A. I. (1988) *Zone Therapy.* Saffron Walden: C. W. Daniel.

Longhorn, F. (1992) *A Sensory Curriculum for very special people.* London: Souvenir Press.

McInnes and Treffry (1982) *Deaf Blind Infants and Children.* Toronto: University of Toronto Press.

Norman, L. (1988) *The Reflexology Hand Book.* London: Guild Publishing.

Tanner, R. (1990) *Step by Step Reflexology.* Croydon: Douglas Barry.

CHAPTER 6

Working with Families of Dual Sensory Impaired Children: a Professional Perspective

June Allen

The importance of parents and educators working together in partnership is well acknowledged throughout literature relating to children with Special Educational Needs. Early educational intervention is dependent upon the development of relationships which consider parents to be instrumental in assessment procedures and in the development of educational programmes. There is a need for a greater examination of the practicalities and responsibilities of such a partnership.

The terms 'parents' and 'families' are often used interchangeably by those considering the social context of the child with Special Needs. It is crucial in the education of dual sensory impaired children that educators perceive the importance of the immediate and extended family. There are two major reasons for this. The first is that everyone who cares for and interacts with the dual sensory impaired child needs to have an understanding of and practical commitment to specific approaches in communication if these are to be effective for the child. The second reason is that parents do not exist in a vacuum with their disabled child: siblings and extended family are inextricable parts of the day-to-day process of care and education. The whole family is the focus of parental concern. For some, close friends fulfil the roles of extended family, and need to be included in perceptions of family life. In order for professionals to accomplish a supportive role with parents they must have a realistic view of family culture and develop a position of credibility within families.

Historically, parents of deafblind children have had to accept inappropriate educational provision, settle for long travelling times to schools not in their own locality, or accept residential school placements.

They have felt uninvolved in the assessment process which determines the child's educational provision and frustrated at the displaced social environment of the child (Furneaux, 1988). Concerns for appropriate educational provision are inextricably entwined with assessment practice and the involvement of parents in that process.

In September 1992 I was appointed one of the Advisory Teachers in the GEST 29 (19) Project for Deaf-Blind children. The work has been aimed towards;

1. promoting and developing specific approaches in educational assessment and provision for early years dual sensory impaired children;

2. supporting their families; and

3. identifying the broader group of dual sensory impaired children with additional disabilities in order to provide advice and support which would enhance existing educational provision.

It has become important to me during this time to begin clarifying ideas about partnership – in particular *why* working together is so important and *how* to promote and encourage a quality of partnership which can be valued by parents and professionals alike. The accumulative experiences of my previous and current roles as a teacher of children with a range of learning difficulties and as a teacher of children with dual sensory impairments led me to believe that it is difficult to make generalisations about what constitutes a qualitative relationship with parents which relates specifically to categories of disability. Dual sensory impairment may give focus to the detail of learning programmes, but relationships with parents are based upon an acknowledgement of individual circumstances. The detail of programmes may be a focus for forming relationships, but it might also for some families be the final stage in a process, arrived at because of a trusting dialogue which has overtly considered other issues within the family. Attempting to unravel what happens between us as professionals and families working together is a complicated business. At one level, we are simply people learning to get along with one other. At another we each have a wealth of knowledge, information and experience which we need to share. At the centre is a child who is the constant focus of all our attentions. There is an immense amount that has to happen before that child can reap the benefits of the potential partnership. The child, the family and the professional need to be considered in the light of policy and the development of practice.

Policy and guidelines

In 1989, the Department of Education and Science produced a document representing policy for deafblind education, which acknowledged the need for parents to be actively involved in assessment procedures and the design of educational programmes (para 10). Emphasis was placed upon the demonstration of educational approaches within the family setting (para 16). It stated also that as the child reaches the age of two years old, Local Education Authorities should have involvement with agencies providing parent counselling (para 12) (DES, 1989).

In 1994, the *Code of Practice on the Identification and Assessment of Special Educational Needs* (DFE, 1994a) stated as a fundamental principle that partnership between parents, children, schools, Local Education Authorities, and other agencies is necessary to secure effective assessment and provision (para 1:2), and that it is the combination of parents' feelings, knowledge, views and anxieties which contribute to a realistic assessment process (para 2:28). The Code acknowledges that some parents are not yet able to become involved in the early years because of the personal impact of disability, and asserts the need for a working partnership based upon openness and confidence between educators and parents (para 2:29). It suggests that assessment should be carried out where the young child and family are comfortable and identifies access to family centres, play opportunities and toy libraries as being effective strategies. (para 5:2)

These issues receive further clarification in the Department For Education pamphlet, *Special Educational Needs – A Guide For Parents* (DFE 1994b), where the 'knowledge, views and experience' of parents are again described as being 'vital', and access to decision making processes reiterated. Parents are encouraged to make use of pre-school strategies such as home visits, home based learning schemes, playgroups, and access to other parents.

The needs of the child

The long and short term needs of the dual sensory impaired child are not essentially different from the needs of other children – to be in touch with the world; to be active and fulfilled within that world; to communicate with people; to enjoy a range of experiences; to express emotions; to be an individual; to be part of a group; to enjoy material objects. Without the learning tools of distance vision and hearing, the child's needs become prioritised and practical access to experiences vital.

The education of dual sensory impaired children is characterised by the methods used to link the child with the environment. These methods have been most clearly refined and documented by those working in the field of deafblindness.

The relationship between the mother and child is the first set of clues educators have in identifying the needs of the child with the combined impairments of hearing and vision. The primary relationship and the attachment (bonding) is dependent upon the use of the senses (the face, the voice, touching). How mother and child feel is communicated to each other and the child learns the effectiveness of his own communicative signals. Understanding the meanings which pass between mother and child is crucial to an understanding of the child.

Jan van Dijk's (1989) development of approaches in the education of deafblind children begins here. Basing his ideas upon his work with rubella children, he believes that problems of management happen early because parents are stressed about the conditions of their children. Eye contact, crucially important in the development of relationships, will not be evident for babies with severe visual disorders; severe auditory impairments deny adequate compensation through hearing; touch becomes the child's route towards interpreting the world and seeking security. Young infants are given security by the ways in which they are handled. From the safety of a mother's arms, the child learns to express an interest in a changing environment (Bowlby, 1982). Where experiences are too intense or irregular, the child will withdraw from exploration (Salzen, 1979).

Touching, unless it is properly considered in relation to the deafblind child's specific needs, can lead to a chaotic and frightening world. It may be other activities which provide comfort for the child, and stereotyped behaviours might emerge. Van Dijk suggests that successful early intervention with specialist techniques will influence relationships and behaviours of the child. He also raises the unanswerable question of whether this can in turn affect the perceived cognitive abilities of the child. He encourages educators and parents to acknowledge that for a deafblind child a 'fully secure base' is understandably lacking, and that educators should seek to develop:

1. ways of assessing mother and child interactions;

2. ways of measuring effectiveness of early intervention programmes;

3. theoretical approaches to the prevention of problems.

It is the contention of many practitioners working in the field that observations of the child's interactions with *all* family members will provide a broad base of information which can potentially contribute to assessing the child's abilities and that the contribution of fathers should particularly be encouraged. The underpinning principles of van Dijk's developing theories – which relate to making sense of the world through enhanced attention to quality of touch, identifying meaningful communication, encouraging the child to understand how to control events, establishing routine and familiarity of people and events, using co-activity to provide a framework for communication – have significant and crucial implications for family life.

Among the basic assumptions driving McInnes and Treffry (1982) in their approaches is that the multi sensory deprived child must have a programme that 'extends over twenty four hours per day, seven days per week and 365 days per year'. In short, providing learning opportunities needs to become a way of life. Parental involvement is perceived by McInnes and Treffry to be essential because parents know the child best and can represent the day-to-day reality of family life. It is within positive family settings that any child is most likely to exhibit abilities. The involvement of families is seen to be crucial, therefore, in the development of effective communication.

For a child with the combined impairments of distance vision and hearing (whether or not this is accompanied by other physical and/or learning difficulties, and whether or not such loss is sensori-neural or conductive) parents and professionals are faced with major difficulties – how to access the whole world to a child who exists within a very small close-to-the-body space and how to prevent the child from being overwhelmed or frightened by that world. These children need to be provided with sensitive access to a world which others find more easily

For dual sensory impaired children intervention strategies need to be established at the earliest possible age, in order that the child's meaningful communication is identified and developed and so that the child will be encouraged to use and develop residual vision and hearing. Concerns exist that children can be further disabled by the solitary nature of their existence to such an extent that difficulties will emerge which dominate behaviour and learning. The extent to which theoretical approaches are based upon consistency is in itself a complete argument for the necessity of parents and educators working together across the child's environ-ments. It is parents and extended family in the home, teachers and nursery nurses in pre-school provision and schools, who implement the work with the children and know the day-to-day realities of the child.

Educators practising in the area of dual sensory impairment develop provision from a core of basic principles. The physical and social environ-ment should be systematically brought within reach of the child; the events and experiences should be offered consistently, with order and routine of people, place and event; systematic attention should be paid to the communicative needs of the child; familiarity facilitates the learning process; attention should be paid to quality of visual, auditory and tactile stimuli; children who develop an understanding of objects require that the objects be used in ways which give reference to event and experience.

Consistent and familiar intervention strategies implemented in consistent and familiar environments by consistent and familiar people do not happen just because they are required and formulated. Rather they emerge because they are given value and importance and are believed to be useful. They are the results of a shared approach which takes into account and makes use of the concerns, observations and ideas of those involved. Evaluation and discussion form a natural part of an honest dialogue.

At the heart of educational concerns lies the child's need to communicate effectively, to participate in family life, and to be a valued member of a social group. Commitment needs to be made to the demonstration of practical approaches through which the child's abilities are drawn out, celebrated and built upon.

The needs of the family

The needs of the child become focused in the provision which can be made. Children with special educational needs are entitled to help from a great number of professional sources. Innumerable professionals conduct innumerable services designed to help the child. Whether or not they do help is largely dependent upon the quality of relationship both with the child and with the parent. Families soon decide for themselves who is useful, who they can manage and when. Involvement may not be dependent upon professional roles – it may be as simple as who parents are comfortable with and who they can talk to.

The implications for parents and families should be considered at every stage of the child's development. They need also to be considered from the varying standpoints of each family member. Professional concerns for the education of the dual sensory impaired child inevitably include consideration of how to work alongside families in ways which are beneficial and acceptable to them, with mutual understanding and trust, and without intrusion into the personal and private domain of home and family. The relationship between parent and professional determines the level to which they can construct a learning environment together, which is balanced, appropriate and based upon an holistic and knowledgeable understanding of the child. It is characterised by the ways which can be found to meaningfully explore and evaluate educational approaches.

Early intervention strategies can only be achieved with the full involvement of parents. Parents are not only concerned with the disabled child, but with their own relationships and feelings, those of their other children and the extended family. The mother of the dual sensory impaired child is usually the greatest learning factor in the child's early years and she needs help and support to maintain positive approaches, both from within the family and from other outside sources. If the whole family needs support toward methods of handling the child, providing activities and developing effective communication with the child (McInnes and Treffry, 1982; Freeman, 1971), then the family needs to be considered in its own right.

It is important for professionals to understand and acknowledge without prejudice the nature of the families they want to develop a partnership with and to recognise that the dual sensory impaired child lives alongside others who have their own needs and requirements. Professional understanding of the impact of the disabled child upon the family is likely to be contributory in quality of relationship between parent and professional.

Stewart and Pollack (1991) carried out research with families of children with wide-ranging disabilities including multiple handicaps and sensory impairments. Their work was concerned with counselling families of young disabled children on a monthly basis over periods between one and three years, and they used a model of bereavement to describe the emotional issues which emerge as parents come to terms with the disabilities of their children. Many of the emotions which they identified have direct implications for professionals attempting to initiate contact, e.g. denial that the child is disabled; anger at the professionals who gave diagnosis or at each other; personal guilt; selectiveness in meeting other parents. They express concern for the complexities of self image in families and in particular for siblings, who they perceive 'often bear the brunt of the stigma in the community'. They ask that the range of professionals involved throughout the child's life be aware of the complexities inherent in family life, and not underestimate the emotional task of dealing with grief and adjusting to loss .

Le Poidevin's model of adjustment to loss in families of disabled children (1985) highlights the need for an understanding that families are affected by disability in every area of their lives, from the overt and practical day-to-day living within families and society, to deeply significant levels of psychological and spiritual grief.

In representing and pursuing notions of partnership it is important to clarify that professionals are committed philosophically and practically to working alongside families with the intention that involvement might potentially enhance quality of life for the whole family, therefore implicitly for the child who is the focus of educational care. Whatever intentions exist, however, the level of involvement is completely dependent upon what a family wants, what constitutes the required professional role, and whether/how we manage to develop a dialogue which will clarify our mutual positions in relation to the child.

The needs of the professional

In effecting practices which elevate the knowledge and experience of parents and families it is vitally important to reflect upon the differently negotiated position the professional holds. The elevation of parents in educational processes does not diminish the importance of the professional point of view. Professionals, too, need to feel that their experience and knowledge are valued and respected and their input welcomed. Partnership in itself requires a fresh look at personal interactive skills and attitudes.

In order to make any achievement in this direction there has to be acknowledgement between us that professionals are first and foremost people simply responding to other people, and secondly specialists responding to the situations which comprise a professional 'workload'. We need to be realistic in perceptions of our own value. The relationship of professional to parent requires each of us to consider not only the purpose of the dialogue but also the style and ease with which we make ourselves available to each other (Cusworth, 1993).

All educational work depends on building relationships and using relationships to facilitate change. Training and experience give teachers a wealth of previous knowledge which is further developed in every new educational experience. Working with a family can be a new and enriching experience. Teachers cannot assume usefulness to a family, however, simply because of training, experience or commitment.

Being selected to help by members of a family, being given access to family life, being trusted and valued are without doubt the privileges of professional practice. In my own experience, most professionals working toward early intervention strategies are anxious to avoid overloading families with their own input and duplicating the advice and support of others. Partnership between professionals themselves has an intrinsic influence on families. Where effective processes exist for professionals to share ideas and strategies and give one another information about their work with children and families, a more sensitive network of support will exist.

Educators are not generally trained counsellors, but many teachers consider that in working with parents there are often situations where counselling skills are a requirement in relationships with parents and children. The negotiation of relationships will be influenced by how professionals respond – how much they listen, how accepting they are, how well they understand barriers, and to what extent they consider their own attitudes, behaviour, and language. The key aspects of the counselling relationship between parents and professionals are described by Cunningham and Davis (1985) as respect, genuineness, attending, getting parents to talk, empathy and the skill to challenge. By establishing and developing relationships which engender these qualities they claim that together parents and professionals will negotiate a clearer model for change through setting goals for the child and developing and evaluating strategies.

Quality of partnership

Partnership is a term which implies sharing, mutual interests and aims and working together to achieve them. In the parent/professional relationship, the establishment of partnership necessitates that emphasis be *taken* away from the weight and density of professional expertise, which is often inaccessible to parents, and *given* to the development of shared understanding, which acknowledges the experience and expertise of parents. Specialist approaches to the child are needed. Professionals can help to introduce these approaches only when they understand the nature of the child's key relationships, the framework for living which already exists for the child, the issues within the family which drive and dominate their day-to-day life, and the expectations which the family have for the child and for themselves.

The contributions which members of the child's family make should be raised in status through clear and overt acknowledgement. The issues which families raise as being important should never be ignored or forgotten. Professionals need to be clear about what is asked for and expected of them, and what they are not qualified or experienced to assist with. These ideas are explored by those working with the families of the deafblind children using the same philosophical underpinning in relation to families as to the child themselves, that is by considering 'locus of control' theory. A child develops the internal locus of control when he begins to feel able to control the events within the environment (van Dijk, 1989).

Ceccarani and Nisi (1989) at the Lega del Fila d'Oro in Italy described the change in their model of working with parents. Initially they perceived parents to be 'change agents' because they implemented strategies which were designed and provided by professionals ('experts'). Parents learned specific responses for specific problems, but had difficulty in resolving new or unexpected issues. They were dependent upon professional intervention and so the locus of control remained external to the family. An altered approach identified the parents as 'learning technologists', who would study and learn basic principles and use this theoretical knowledge to develop methodology. In this way families were supported toward decision making and choosing what they describe as 'lines of conduct'.

Cunningham and Davis (1985), in their analysis of the relationship between professionals and the parents of children with special educational needs, assert the need to establish **collaboration.** They suggest that partnership is defined by the ways in which experience, rights and responsibilities are perceived between individuals, and they contrast 'expert' and 'transplant' models with a 'consumer' model to illustrate these notions. Simplistically, in the first, the professional takes control and makes decisions while parents follow instructions; in the second, parents learn specific skills from the professionals and implement them; in the third the parents are considered to be more informed about their situation and in control of decision making. The third model describes a relationship founded upon honesty and confidence, within which parent and professional negotiate, information flows both ways, parents rights are paramount, and professional responsibilities are geared toward listening, understanding and providing alternatives. Thus the 'consumer' model qualifies partnership.

Building relationships with parents and families

Talking and listening

Parents themselves will outline their own specific and individual needs in relation to their dual sensory impaired child. When they are clear about what professionals have and are able to offer, they will clarify and negotiate what is useful to them. All professionals are equipped with their own agendas – at worst, some of our questions and observations can be difficult, pre-emptive, loaded, intrusive. In attending to the realities of family life we can be helped towards a more temperate and balanced view of our own roles.

The talking and listening which happens to establish relationships between parents and professionals may encompass the full range of life issues about the child (feeding, sleeping, relationships, communication, behaviour, physical and emotional development, etc.) They may wish to discuss related issues which affect their perceptions of the child in any of these areas (the specific requirements of their other children at mealtimes, the amount of attention needed for one child while siblings lose out, the difficulties of depending on families or friends for basic or supplementary care, the impact of the attitudes of others to the child, etc.) Most important to remember is that for families the issues around the child are vivid, emotional and full time. What they feel and the transmission of those feelings to their child (Jurgens, 1977) is the single most important element of communication. Professionals can represent an objectively useful standpoint. What parents and children say provides crucial clues to professional understanding. Particularly in the early stages of intervention they are collecting information which helps them to piece together a realistic picture of the child's life. They need to do this at a pace which is acceptable to parents and in ways which are unthreatening. They need also to participate in a dialogue which considers their own professional standpoint without unreasonable emphasis and without creating new demands for the family, by reinforcing points of accessibility and encouraging negotiation.

Observing and demonstrating

Approaches to dual sensory impaired children are grounded in practical approaches. The development of educational strategies is centred in observation of the child's meaningful communication. Watching the child in a variety of situations, structured and unstructured across environments, provides information about residual vision and hearing. This information forms a framework for establishing routine and consistency and for the systematic introduction of change. By establishing what the child already knows and responds to best, educators are able to build on existing learning and natural interactions. An understanding of established familial practices and the introduction of educational strategies are both most effectively achieved through demonstration. Professional working with the child must be complementary, not an overtly alternative model for living or interacting .

Educators watching parents and parents watching educators with the child provide an experimental framework and a knowledgeable base for going forward. Observing each other in the demonstration of approaches to the child equalises the importance of our mutual contributions. To work together, positively engaging the child in practical activity, provides a strong link between family and professional practice, but more importantly, perhaps, a direct and unquestionable link between environments. There exists also the opportunity to frame immediate and mutually interested questions and answers relating specifically to practice with the child. In this way the abilities of the child are recognised, observation and discussion lead to the development of strategy, and existing strategies are evaluated. When the process is repeated it is built upon. Mutual engagement in activity also provides opportunities for parents and educators to value precise and strategic interactive techniques alongside relaxed and informal interactions.

The use of video recording for analysing both the child's reactions and the effects of the adult's interventions is well established in approaches to dual sensory impaired children and provides an invaluable focus for discussion. This method of close observation can only be satisfactorily achieved when parent and professional both feel safe to be watched and are secure in the knowledge that the critical and analytical eye is focused clearly upon celebrating achievement and solving problems – not being discovered to be wrong.

Observing and demonstrating leads towards a greater understanding of theoretical standpoints, and professional accountability.

Working together

Implicit in the approaches being described is the notion that parent and professional working together for the child with a dual sensory impairment will naturally participate in processes which determine appropriate educational provision and placement. Collecting information, making decisions together, designing and evaluating programmes, achieving accessible record keeping and testing the use and effectiveness of resources are the requirements of a precise and accurate assessment of the child's needs.

Practical implications

Routes into partnership with parents and families need to be considered flexibly and creatively. If parents and professionals are to work together, conditions need to be created whereby they are comfortable in doing so. Children, parents and families have different requirements at different times and a range of provision which offers choice is likely to facilitate involvement. A range of variables needs to be considered even before the purpose and content of the dialogue.

Location

The location of any dialogue between professional and parent can be potentially crucial. In pre-school provision, home visiting and home-based learning schemes are now well established in many areas. Some parents may welcome professionals into their homes, other may not. Some parents may find it easy to attend institutional settings or resource centres, others may not. Once the dialogue is established it becomes easier to negotiate location according to its differing purposes, but in the early stages parents need to be in a place which is comfortable to them and it is they who will indicate where this is once a choice is available.

Working with the child in the home environment allows professionals to experience first hand the physical and social environment within which the child's early learning happens. It allows for highly individual and intensive interactions between professionals and families. In the child's familiar and principal learning environment, professionals are most likely to observe achievements and abilities which form the basis of initial and ongoing assessment. Observing the child with mother, father, brothers and sisters will give a great deal of information about how, when and why the child is communicating and using residual vision and hearing. Introducing new stimuli or different approaches is more likely to be acceptable to the child with the involvement of family members. Within the safe and familiar context of home, changes can be made most easily. When the family contribute to and are implicitly involved in the reasoning and decision-making processes which facilitate change, they are more likely to reinforce educational approaches between visits. Because they are involved, they in turn are more likely to assist in the process of observing the child's responses and evaluating the success of stimuli and altered approaches. Work in the home might represent the least upheaval within the family. On the other hand, parents might not want a professional procession intruding on to their territory. They might not wish observations to be carried out so close to family life. This is their prerogative. There are many reasons why professionals and parents may prefer or require working together outside the home environment. These are more extensively explored by Cunningham and Davis (1985), who evidence the need for locational issues to be considered very seriously.

It is as important for professional services to include the provision of neutral territory which is welcoming, friendly and accessible to families, where it is possible to work on an individual basis and where educational processes can be discussed and demonstrated. Nurseries, schools or specialist centres offer a wealth of human and physical resources which can enhance the dialogue between parent and professional and provide a focus for activity. Care should be taken that wherever the locational setting of playgroups, toy libraries, workshops, nurseries, classrooms and meetings are, they do not represent the province of professionals more than the province of the child or family. Initiatives which encourage parents and families to meet each other and/or professionals away from the home need to concentrate upon what qualities constitute a safe and comfortable environment.

The presence of children

Working together with the disabled child is crucial in the collection of information and in developing strategies toward educational programmes. It is also crucial to the demonstration of programmes and in evaluating progress. It is useful also to include siblings and extended family in these processes. To have children present may be particularly helpful in providing the focus of attention and a constant grounding in the practicalities. But the presence of children may also be distracting where parents and professionals need to listen to each other, to talk about arising issues and to make decisions together, or to talk about issues indirectly associated with the child. The care of the children in these situations needs to be considered. Professional support may need to include organised care and activities which the parents are confident of accepting, both for their disabled child and for other children in the family, notably pre-school children. Not all parents want or need this, but many do and the availability is often a deciding factor in attendance for meetings or workshops.

Availability of transport

Many families need support with transport. The provision of transport can be a great incentive for parents to attend meetings and workshops. Sensitive provision which considers the quality of transport and the individual requirements of children and families is always a consideration when locations outside the home are offered.

Time

A constant factor throughout all the ideas and practices expressed in this chapter is time. Neither parents nor professionals ever have enough time to satisfy their own perceptions of what the child and one another need. Establishing relationships, talking and listening, observing and demonstrating, working together, all takes time and the time it takes is variable for each individual circumstance. It is essential that what time we have is characterised by its quality.

Group support

Whilst emphasis has been placed here on the dialogue between individual families and professionals, increasing attention is now being paid to the value of working with groups of parents. It is clear that parents need to talk to one another and that it is they who ultimately give one another most support.

Ceccarani and Nisi (1989) describe a training programme within which five of six sets of parents are encouraged to meet together on a six monthly basis for personal and group discussions. They assert the need to include siblings and grandparents. Specific issues are selected, and by identifying and analysing problems with one another and professionals, parents are perceived to learn how to find their own resolutions. The training is evaluated by the use of a range of questionnaires, before and after the sessions. One explores the feelings of parents towards their child and his upbringing. A second considers trust and acceptance of the child, specific problems, relationship issues and attitudes to educational approaches. A third compares ways of dealing with specific situations, by using a 'before and after' training approach.

Termly parent weekends at the Centre for Deaf-Blind education in France also seek to include friends alongside parents, grandparents and siblings. During the two days participants can experience small group discussions and videos focusing upon issues directly relating to their children, educational activities with the child, specific training groups (e.g. signing), free time, communal meals, consultation with medical practitioners, parent meetings and an assessment of the weekend (Gimenes, 1989.)

In this country Sense Family Weekends periodically provide a range of workshops and discussion groups, with creche facilities for children. The overt consideration of the whole family and the balance of activity (parents with professionals, parents without professionals, parents with children, parents without children, in concentrated and fluid activity, through educational or domestic situations) provide an accessible route to the development of a truer partnership.

These models of working have much to offer educators concerned with the broader groups of dual sensory and multi sensory impaired children and it is evident that parents have enthusiastically welcomed such approaches. It is not always possible for educators to organise on such a scale. It is useful, however, to use these approaches in an attempt to distil the qualities of working partnerships, since they are exemplary in promoting the practice of successfully building relationships and considering the practical implications of working with families.

References

Bowlby, J. (1982) *Attachment and Loss.* vol 1. USA: Basic Books.

Ceccarani, P. and Nisi, A. (1989) 'The parent training programme destined to parents of children who present serious behavioural and psychological problems', in Best, A.B. (ed) *Papers on the education of the deaf-blind: proceedings of the Warwick Conference.* Birmingham: IAEDB.

Cunningham, C. and Davis, H. (1985) *Working with parents: frameworks for collaboration.* Milton Keynes: OUP.

Cusworth, S. (1993) 'Parents and professionals – adversaries, opponents, bedfellows or allies', *Information Exchange*, **39**, 16-17.

Department of Education and Science (1989) *Educational Provision for Deaf-blind Children.* London: HMSO.

Department for Education (1994a) *Code of Practice on the Identification and Assessment of Special Educational Needs.* London: HMSO.

Department for Education (1994b) *Special Educational Needs – A Guide For Parents.* London: HMSO.

90

Freeman, P. (1971) *A parents' guide to the early care of the deaf-blind child.* Birmingham: Sense.

Furneaux, B. (1988) *Special parents.* Milton Keynes: Open University Press.

Gimenes, R. (1989) 'Parents' weekends: a termly meeting at Larnay. A four-year collaboration between parent and professionals', in Best, A.B. (ed) *Papers on the education of the deaf-blind: proceedings of the Warwick Conference.* Birmingham: IAEDB.

Jurgens, M.R. (1977) *Confrontation between the young deaf-blind child and the outside world.* Netherlands: Swets and Zeitlinger..

Le Poidevin, S. and Cameron, J. (1985) 'Is there more to Portage than education?', in Paly, B., Addington, G., Kerfoot, S. and Sigston, A. *Portage – the importance of parents.* Windsor: NFER-Nelson.

McInnes, J. M. and Treffry, J.A. (1982) *Deaf-blind infants and children – a developmental guide.* London: University of Toronto Press.

Salzen, E.A. (1979) 'Social attachment and a sense of security', in von Crannich, M., Foppa, K., Lepenies, W. and Ploog, D. *Human Ethnography: claims and limits of a new discipline.* Cambridge: Cambridge University Press.

Stewart, J. and Pollack, G. (1991) *A bereavement model for working with families of handicapped children.* London: Children's Society

van Dijk, J. (1989) 'The Sint Michielsgestel approach to diagnosis and education of multisensory impaired persons', in Best, A.B. (ed) *Papers on the education of the deaf-blind: proceedings of the Warwick Conference.* Birmingham: IAEDB.

CHAPTER 7

The Training and Role of Intervenors in One Region of Britain

Jonathan Griffiths

Multi-handicapped sensory impairments (which include dual sensory impairment) are perhaps the least understood of disabilities, and the most traumatic to the individual. It has been stated that the cross-developmental effects of a combined sensory loss cannot be underestimated. That which is not taught, often through touch, will not be learnt. The dual sensory impaired child rarely has his educational needs met in provision catering for children who are hearing impaired or in provision for children who are visually impaired. The more multi-disabled the child the less likely it is that the child will be able to access any learning situation without a rigorous degree of outside assistance. Ideally this assistance should be available as soon as the child is diagnosed as having a combination of sensory impairments. It is at the time of initial diagnosis that the family needs the most support as in

> ... the early years, the infant will always be close at hand throughout its waking hours. Few other handicaps are so totally demanding of mother and other members of the family. In the early years the dual sensory impaired infant will not be able to amuse itself, and will require constant manipulation and conscious planned effort on the part of the family to develop both concepts and communication. It is little wonder that when adequate support for the infant and its family is not available, the choice of early institutionalisation is forced upon the family. (McInnes and Treffry, 1982)

Attendance at the Second Canadian Conference on the Education of the Deafblind, held at W Ross Macdonald School in March 1986, introduced the author to the Canadian concept of Intervention as a method of support for children who are dual sensory impaired in a variety of settings. John McInnes stated at the Conference that 'the concept of intervention is at the same time simple and yet complex – apparently easy to introduce and yet extremely difficult to apply, a label that can be tacked onto anything and yet often a description of nothing'. (McInnes, 1986).

Intervention, as viewed in Canada, appeared to enable the dual sensory impaired child to integrate more fully into its educational and social environment. In Ontario intervention, at least at this stage, was available to children both in school and at home. It was possible for the author to visit children who are dual sensory impaired and who had intervenors appointed to work with them and to see them in both the school and home environments.

The concept of intervention was, therefore, seen as a particularly appropriate one for assistance in the development of children who had damage to their distance senses of hearing and vision. These children need particular, specialised help as they have been unable to assimilate those areas of development which occur naturally in children without those impairments. For various reasons, most of them to do with finance, it was not felt possible to 'import' the Canadian model of intervention in its entirety and use it in the United Kingdom.

Having successfully applied for funding from central government for the development of regional provision for the education of deafblind children, the consortium of Local Education Authorities led by Staffordshire and including Shropshire and Hereford & Worcester decided to adopt intervention as their model of support for their children who are dual sensory impaired and who attend schools for children with severe learning difficulties. Of the three authorities in this particular consortium, only Staffordshire was employing a teacher of multi-sensory impaired (MSI) children. The teacher concerned was supporting these children in their existing schools. The other two authorities conducted an audit of the children in their respective schools for children with severe learning difficulties and discovered the small numbers of dual sensory impaired children that were to be expected in the schools. Figures accepted in other parts of the developed world, and in particular Holland and the Nordic countries, would suggest a prevalence of something in the order of 0.018 per cent or 1 in 6,000 of the school population.

The audit of provision was undertaken by the author who used as his basis for research a set of criteria for the identification of deafblind children, previously adopted by the Education Psychology Service of Birmingham LEA (see Figure 7.1). The numbers of children identified as a result of the audit showed that in Shropshire there were five and possibly six children aged two to eight years attending Shropshire schools for children with severe learning difficulties. In Hereford & Worcester it appeared that there were ten children within the authority who could be identified as being dual sensory impaired or, using the terms of the survey, deafblind. The Shropshire figure included one child of pre-school age and the Hereford & Worcester figure included four children of pre-school age. Hereford & Worcester also had one child placed out-county in specialist provision for children who are deafblind.

Multi-sensory impaired, deaf-blind children: Survey, 1992.

Please identify the numbers of children in your school who individually display AT LEAST SIX of the following characteristics:

1. **Sensory Impairment** (must exhibit both)
Has a significant degree of visual and hearing impairment.
Has a combined sensory impairment which is preventing progressive development.

2. **Communication Implications**
Has no access currently to speech and, therefore, requires augmented forms of communication.
Requires alternative teaching methods to those normally in use in school.

3. **Educational Observations**
Has the potential for movement/ambulance (aided or unaided).
Stands out as being 'different' from current class group.
Displays 'hidden potential'.

4. **Exclusions**
Is not Down's syndrome or Usher's syndrome.

Number of Children
Nursery   Primary   Secondary

This survey form was used with the kind permission of the City of Birmingham Education Department Psychology Service.

Figure 7.1 Criteria for the identification of deafblind children

The geographical spread of both the schools and their populations, combined with the predominantly rural nature of the area, meant that any form of unit provision was likely to prove unworkable. The concept of intervention had been implicit in their bid for funding and this was the way the consortium decided to proceed once the audits had been completed. The idea was that the children identified would need extra help in order to integrate more fully into their existing educational provision. It was considered that the provision of additional trained teaching staff to support the identified children would prove to be too much of a financial burden on the individual LEAs for the project to have any realistic hope of continuing beyond the three year life of the government funding. Intervention was seen as a viable alternative and it was thought that, if the project proved to be successful within the three authority areas, there was more chance of the support continuing after the grants ran out.

Definition of the role of the intervenor

In order that the role of the intervenor within this consortium was understood by all those involved in the project, i.e. teachers, classroom assistants, headteachers, support services and local authority officers, it was deemed essential that a definition of the role of the intervenor should be developed and adopted by the consortium as a whole. By December 1992 the following had been agreed by all three authorities:

Intervention - definition and role

An intervenor provides individual support for the deaf-blind child to enable effective communication and the receipt of clear information. The role of the intervenor is to enable the child to take full advantage of learning and social experiences and to gain fuller access to the environment and the schools curriculum.

In conjunction with other professionals and the family the intervenor's role concerns assistance with all areas of learning including:

- providing opportunities for the child to gain access to the curriculum
- assisting in the implementation of a programme of sensory stimulation
- assisting in the development of an appropriate communication system
- assisting in the promotion of independence activities, i.e. feeding, mobility, etc.

- providing opportunities for the child to make choices and decisions

- providing appropriate opportunities and motivation for social interaction

This work will involve the intervenor in:

- working in close co-operation with other professionals to promote the transfer of specialist skills and activities between different situations encountered by the child and family

- maintaining simple records to assist with the assessment of the child's ability and progress

- assisting with the organisation and supervision of group curricular activities outside the classroom, i.e. swimming, educational visits, etc.

This definition owed much to the Canadian approach but also drew on the individual experiences of those people most closely involved with the project in the three authorities and from the voluntary sector. Increasing awareness showed that the educational needs of this particular group of disadvantaged children could best be met through a form of support not currently used as a matter of policy within any local authority area of the United Kingdom.

The appointment of intervenors

As soon as the funding cycle commenced in April 1992 it was deemed important that individuals, who were to be called intervenors, would be appointed to identified children as soon as possible. This was accomplish-ed first in Staffordshire, which, as has already been mentioned, employed a support teacher who had gained the qualification to teach children who are multi-sensory impaired and was working in the authority's schools for children with severe learning difficulties. This support teacher had identi-fied five children within these schools who she felt were dual sensory impaired and should receive some enhanced form of support. It was these children who received the first people appointed as intervenors, within a matter of weeks of the project starting.

In Staffordshire the local authority advertised for their initial group of intervenors and then appointed further intervenors as a result of their experience with this first group. Appointment came after advertising for people to work to job and person specifications similar to those for special support assistants working with children with visual and hearing impairments. At interview it was emphasised that the ability to form a relationship with an individual child was of vital importance and the ability to understand the concept of nurturance was judged to be essential. In many cases it was left to the judgement of the interviewing panel, as such attributes are very difficult to identify in a formal situation; the intuition of the interviewing panel was critical in this area. The intervenors had to be aware that the development of communication skills, both on their part and with the children they would be working with, was to be of the utmost importance. Other key elements that were required of the people wishing to be intervenors were adaptability; an ability to use their initiative; the ability to work as part of a team, but have a different role from the usual members of such a team; and the ability to communicate within the team and to visiting professionals who would all be making contributions to the programmes for each child. They had to express an interest in their own professional development as it was envisaged that some form of training additional to the initial intervenor training mentioned later would be offered and undertaken.

The relationship that the intervenors were expected to develop with the children was seen as vital and it was hoped that, especially with children of pre-school age who were perhaps attending school on a part-time basis, they would be able to develop a relationship with the parents and perhaps foster and enhance the links between the home and the school. In the case of one of the intervenors appointed in Staffordshire to a child of Punjabi-speaking parents, who herself had the same mother-tongue, the links formed were quite spectacular, to the extent of enabling the mother, who spoke no English, to visit the school for the first time.

When the child to whom the intervenor was to be appointed was of pre-school age, and this happened in a number of cases across the authorities, it was felt essential that the parents of the children concerned should be as involved as possible in the selection of the intervenor who was to work with their child. The parents had to feel at ease with both the concept of intervention and the person who was going to attempt to implement it with their child. This was a major difference to the procedure in Canada where the parents had almost the ultimate say in the hiring and firing of intervenors working with their children, particularly in the home situation.

At the end of the summer term, 1994, the following numbers of trained intervenors were in post in the three authorities: Staffordshire 11; Hereford & Worcester 6; Shropshire 7.

In Staffordshire the intervenors were appointed to the Sensory Support Service and then allocated to the children. In Hereford & Worcester intervenors were appointed from the school staff; these people were then seconded to the Hereford & Worcester Service for Children with Sensory

Impairments (SCSI) for the duration of the project, thereby ensuring that when the project ended, the schools would be able to retain the expertise of these trained members of staff.

Training of intervenors

As these people appointed as intervenors were acknowledged to have a role that was to be markedly different from any that previously existed in schools, it was considered essential that they receive, as soon after they were appointed as possible, some form of specialist training. By this time work on intervention in Canada had progressed considerably, to the extent that there is now a recognised two year course for the training of intervenors established at George Brown College in Toronto. This course came into being because of the expansion of intervention as a method of supporting dual sensory impaired children and adults within Ontario and was the result of many years of research and development. It was recognised that such a course would not be possible within the three year span of the funding for the project in the United Kingdom. It even proved impossible in the time available to organise a course that would satisfy the criteria for the award of the status of National Vocational Qualification (NVQ). It was decided to work with the voluntary sector, namely RNIB and Sense, who were the major national service providers prior to the project, to set up an 'in-house' training schedule that would satisfy the needs of the consortium.

The initial part of the training for intervenors was a week-long residential course organised and hosted by the Pathways Deafblind Department at RNIB Condover Hall School. During the course the intervenors were expected to shadow a child and to become involved in the classroom activities that the particular child was undertaking. Approximately 60 per cent of the training time was spent in this way. This gave the intervenors the opportunity to begin to develop a relationship with a child, which is continually emphasised as prerequisite for working with any dual sensory impaired child. The intervenors also had the opportunity to talk with teachers and those other staff in the department who undertake an intervenor-type role. Time was allocated for the trainees to observe work being undertaken with the particular child in the residential setting in the evenings.

During the week tutorial sessions were organised on various aspects of the make-up of the group of children. This included sessions on visual impairment, hearing impairment, communication and multi-sensory impairment. These tutorial sessions were given by different members of the teaching staff group of the department. Much of the information given in the tutorial sessions was instructional in nature and allowed the intervenors to learn about the eye and vision, the ear and hearing, the development of alternative communication strategies and the effects of a combination of sensory impairments on development. Use was made during the whole week of the INSITE Curriculum from the SKI*HI Institute at Utah State University, Department of Communication Disorders. This model (Watkins, 1989) is a training package in home intervention for infant, toddler, and pre-school aged multihandicapped sensory impaired children.

On the last day of the course teachers from the local authority schools to which the intervenors had been appointed were invited to join the intervenors for a seminar day, led by Jenny Fletcher, Head of the Family and Education Services at Sense Midlands. The day covered various aspects of work with dual sensory impaired children and included sessions on definitions, the implications of intervention, the use of the environment, mobility and information on aspects of child care programmes.

Further follow-up training for the intervenors was organised within each authority and included additional work on vision loss and hearing impairment and strategies to alleviate the worst aspects of such losses; work on movement and mobility, as many of the children identified also had physical impairments; information on alternative strategies such as massage and the use of other senses; work on communication with particular emphasis being placed on objects of reference, which were seen as a possible avenue for some of the identified children to acquire a formalised communication system; and some work on the support of staff who are working with delicate children or those whose prognosis is not good.

Throughout the project both the intervenors and the class teachers have been supported by a teacher from one of the respective sensory support services on a regular basis in their schools. The author has also been part of the team undertaking these school visits, about once each term.

Alongside the ongoing training for intervenors it was decided that some form of formalised training should be made available to the teachers who had also had an intervenor working as part of their classroom team, at least for some of the time. An accredited modular course entitled 'An Introduction to Multi-Sensory Impairment' was organised through the Oxford Modular Scheme administered by Westminster College Oxford and validated by Worcester College of Higher Education. The course has two modules: An Introduction to Multi-Sensory Impairment and Communication with Multi-Sensory Impaired Children. Each module consists of a hundred hours study time comprising thirty hours directed study and seventy hours for reading, research and so forth. Each module carries an assignment which the students must undertake in order to obtain their credit towards a Certificate in Professional Studies. Both assignments have to be of an acceptable standard in order for the credit to be awarded. The course was run initially during the spring and summer terms, 1994, and a second presentation took place during the autumn of 1994 and the spring of 1995.

The first cohort was restricted to teachers but the second cohort was opened up to intervenors, provided they hold at least a nursery nurse qualification or have completed another module under the scheme as an access module, or are prepared to use the first module on this course as their access. This avenue was seen as a way for the intervenors to obtain a recognised qualification, as the National Vocational Qualification route was not available to them.

Evaluation

The project in the Staffordshire-led consortium has been evaluated by two students as part of their post-experience studies. The evaluation has looked at the effects intervention is having on the schools in which it is being used and also at any quantifiable effect it is having on the development of the children. There has been little research done anywhere else in the world, but it has been possible to obtain a copy of 'Validation of the Intervenor Method of Providing Direct Services to Deafblind Children in the Home Setting' (SKI*HI Institute, Utah State University, 1993). The research investigates intervention in several areas including development, communication, and the effect on families, and uses an INSITE Checklist and the Callier Azusa Scales together with a control group in other states..

In the area of development of the child the report concludes:

> The 1989-90 data is perhaps the best way to look at the progress of the children. This data uses each child's first and last test during his or her entire time in the program to calculate the PCI (Proportional Change Index). As such, the PCI represents each child's progress during each child's entire treatment time. All PCIs reported in the 1982-92 data are greater than one. This meant that the average child who receives intervenor services makes greater progress during the services than before in all developmental areas.

It further states:

> All domains reported in the 1989-92 data except one (motor development on the Callier Azusa) show actual post-test scores to be greater than or equal to predicted post-test scores. In other words, 93

per cent of the domains show actual post-test scores being higher than predicted post-test scores. The average child who receives Intervenor Services scores higher at post-test time in the large majority of developmental domains than what would be expected due to maturation alone.

And goes on to state:

...children who receive Intervenor Services make greater gains in all developmental domains than what would be expected due to chance (statistical significance). Their post-test scores from a standpoint of educational significance are convincingly greater than their pre-test scores.

One of the conclusions that the report comes to is as follows:

From the data presented...it is evident that Intervenor Services assist children in all developmental areas and result in greater child progress than the progress that is made by the children who do not receive Intervenor Services.

The evaluation reports submitted to the Staffordshire-led GEST consortium examined the project from two different perspectives. Firstly there was a report into the project from the viewpoint of the intervenors and the teachers with whom they worked, and secondly from the viewpoint of the schools who were involved and the project co-ordinators.

The first report produced mostly positive results, particularly with regard to the difference that intervention had made to the work that it was possible to do with the identified child in a particular group:

Five of the teachers felt the intervenors has a closer relationship with the child; communicated more effectively and showed more awareness of how to meet their needs.

Teachers raised a number of positive points for having an intervenor in the classroom. One found the exchanging of ideas useful; another that the child had found it a very positive experience and that it enabled her to be more flexible with the staffing in the group; another also commented on the change in the responses of the child with MSI; the final teacher found the attitude and dedication very motivating for all the staff working with the class group.

Responses from intervenors in this first report (Morgan, 1994) included:

Two intervenors felt that the disruptive behaviour had decreased and the child had become more assertive. One intervenor felt that intervention had significantly reduced behaviour tantrums for the child she works with. Group sessions were much improved, the intervenor went on to explain that she now had the time to explain all that was happening and this was reducing the level of frustration for the child. One intervenor noted a change in visual and auditory response since the start of intervention, 'he is using his vision better...'.

The second report (Jones, 1994) contained among its summary points the following:

All agreed that the use of intervention and intervenors has been of benefit to the education of these pupils.

The importance of a whole school and whole team approach to intervention was highlighted.

The importance of the heightening of awareness for the whole school is stressed.

The second report also highlights concerns for the future of this work and asks questions as to whether any aspects of the project will be able to continue; and thereby hangs the most important question regarding the use of pump-priming and the ability of local education authorities to continue such projects within increasingly limited resources.

The future

There can be little doubt that the project to provide intervention services to a number of dual sensory impaired children in one particular region of the United Kingdom has met with considerable success from the point of view of the developmental progress of the individual children. This progress is difficult to quantify, but observation of the children over the period of the provision of intervention leads to the belief that the effect that intervention has on the development of school-age dual sensory impaired children is remarkably similar to that quoted in the Utah study.

Intervention as a concept for providing support to dual sensory impaired children has been shown to be successful. It is to be hoped that the experiment that has been undertaken in the Staffordshire-led consortium will be allowed to continue in some form with continuing LEA support. The imminent changes to the funding arrangements for special education, whereby special schools are to be in control of their budgets and may even opt out of local authorities themselves, is likely to mitigate against the adoption of intervention on any large scale.

Author's acknowledgements

The author wishes to thank the co-ordinators for deafblind services within the Staffordshire-led consortium for their assistance in writing this chapter and for allowing the author to become involved in such a stimulating project. Thanks are also due to the Pathways Department at RNIB Condover Hall School for allowing use of their Intervenor Course materials; and to the intervenors and the children whose hard work has made the project such a success.

References

Fredericks, H. and Baldwin, V. (1987) 'Individuals with sensory impairments: Who are they?' in Goetz, L., Guess D. and Stremel-Campbell, K. (eds) *Innovative program design for individuals with dual sensory impairments.* Baltimore MD: Brookes.

Freeman, P. (1985) *The deaf-blind baby; A programme of care.* London: Heinemann.

Jones, B. (1994) 'Education of Deafblind Children, Evaluation Report' (unpublished).

McInnes, J. and Treffry, J. (1982) *Deafblind infants and children – a developmental guide.* London: University of Toronto Press.

McInnes, J. (1986) 'Intervention is the Key', *Intervention*, **10**(1).

Morgan, A. (1994) 'Evaluation report on the Staffordshire GEST 29/92 Consortium Project' (unpublished).

Siegal-Causey, E. and Downing, J. (1987) 'Non-symbolic communication development: Theoretical concepts and educational strategies', in Goetz, L., Guess, D. and Stremel-Campbell, K. (eds) *Innovative program design for individuals with dual sensory impairments.* Baltimore MD: Brookes.

SKI*HI Institute (1993) *Validation of the Intervenor Method of Providing Direct Services to Deafblind Children in the Home Setting.* Logan, Utah: Utah State University.

Watkins, S. (ed) (1989) *The INSITE Model – A model of home intervention for infant, toddlers and pre-school aged multihandicapped sensory impaired children.* Logan, Utah: HOPE Inc.

CHAPTER 8

A Consortium Approach to Staff Development

John Kaye and Keith Humphreys

Introduction

In 1992 a consortium of LEAs from the North East of England was successful in applying for DES funding to develop provision for pupils whom it classified as 'deafblind'. The bid was secured in the context of a trend in government education policy which earmarked funding to foster the development of specific initiatives.

At the same time there was also a government-inspired move towards market-driven competition between schools. The drive to raise the quality of education for all pupils is seen within the context of achieving greater efficiency and effectiveness. Value for money is now a key concept. Whilst such approaches are of undoubted benefit to the majority of pupils, low-incidence disability groups are inevitably going to suffer without appropriate protection. This is especially true when it comes to the unit costs involved in financing the professional development of, and harnessing resources for, specialist minority groups of teachers.

For this reason the lessons to be learnt from the initiative described below are both special and of paramount importance.

The North East GEST 29 (14) consortium project

A North East consortium of LEAs established a project under GEST 29 (14) funding which included five local education authorities and a non-maintained special school. They all committed additional resources to the project. This was a unique initiative in its development and management within the educational provision for pupils with special educational needs in the North East of England. It reflected the importance of central government funding as a means of ensuring that educational provision for a low-incidence disability group was developed. It also reflected the importance of regional co-operation by education professionals in order to make appropriate educational provision for minority disability groups. Indeed, it represented a challenge to facilitate collaboration between six organisations which had different management styles and priorities.

The consortium formed a management committee of senior managers whose task was to co-ordinate and delegate responsibility for the development of the whole programme. A project team of qualified teachers and assistants was appointed to implement the provision and was based at the Regional Advisory and Assessment Centre located within the non-maintained special school. Throughout the duration of the project, professional development activity was initiated both across the participating LEAs and with the project team. This chapter is based on information obtained during a formal evaluation of the project and relates to the wide variety of 'deafblind' focused professional development activities carried out in the region over a two-year period. It addresses key issues and asks questions about how provision for other minority groupings can be initiated, delivered and maintained for the effective training of professionals.

The professional development of the project team

The four teachers in the project team were all experienced in different areas relating to education for dual sensory impaired children, but none of them had a specific 'deafblind' qualification. Three had experience of working with pupils with profound and multiple handicap, and one was qualified to teach the visually impaired. They all needed to develop their knowledge and skill in this new specific field but they also needed to develop their ability to work out of school settings both within and across LEA boundaries and in multi-professional contexts. The project co-ordinator was concerned to appreciate the expectations of each of the consortium members. He was aware of tensions both within and beyond the consortium with regard to the impact and nature of the emerging provision. As a consequence of the new LEA-wide responsibilities, the teachers felt uncertain about what was to be expected of them, given their developing knowledge in this emerging field of educational provision.

The project teachers' regional concerns

In general they all felt that their varied experiences in the areas of teaching pupils with severe learning difficulties and sensory impairment was of value. They all felt a strong commitment to work in a collaborative team and to be supportive of one another.

There was a challenge in responding to different needs of LEAs. It was generally recognised that the establishment of new lines of communication between members of the project team and staff in the LEAs was a challenging task that required sensitivity. Each LEA had its own pattern of protocol and within each pattern there were differing points of individual professional expectation. Project advisory teachers found the new 'high profile' that LEA-wide exposure gave them to be very different from the classroom-based pressures in which they were used to working. As a consequence, the project advisory teachers did not find it an easy task to respond to their new co-ordinating roles and responsibilities. The project co-ordinator perceived the challenge differently and recognised the need to work to a clearly defined code of practice across all of the LEAs and the project team. There were clear constraints that had to be observed together with the need for well-disciplined professional practice.

There were different influences emerging on the understanding of a definition of deafblind. The project team had drawn their understanding from a variety of sources including the Nordic and the DFE definitions. There was a feeling that it would be inappropriate at the early stages in the project development to conclude with one definition. It was felt that as they increased their experience so a more pragmatic definition may emerge. Different LEAs maintained their own specific definitions. Some felt that able pupils in mainstream schools should be included, some felt that identification should be restricted to those with severe learning difficulties and some even felt that there was no real need to distinguish the needs of these pupils at all. The adoption of an interpretation of a definition seemed to depend upon either financial implications, existing provision, prior beliefs of the special LEA inspectors, or a commitment to explore the possible need for this new provision. Eventually a broad and all-encompassing definition was adopted that specified a dual dysfunction of sight and hearing but did not attempt to exclude children with additional learning difficulties. LEAs and schools were given the responsibility of how liberally to interpret the term.

The notion of confidentiality had an impact on the professional practice of the project team. They were all aware that they should not make unguarded or 'off the record' comments and that they had to be very careful about making enquiring comments that could be misinterpreted as being informed opinion. This was also of concern when the teachers were working in a multi-professional context. They felt that such a situation could impair the development of professional understanding.

Opportunities for professional development came from a variety of valuable sources. The team identified professional development opportunities that they had attended in the early period of the project. Of these, the visit to a special school for deafblind children in Scotland was perceived to have been particularly successful. From both the perspective of knowledge and a professional application, this was a very highly rated experience. Attendance at the annual 'Weekend Away' organised by Sense was seen to have been valuable. Two of the project teachers visited schools in Denmark and in particular a school specialising in children with dual sensory impairments.

The project teachers' self reflections

In the early stages of the project everyone appeared to be in a very vulnerable state but as the professional development activities increased the teachers' confidence grew to enable them to undertake the tasks more effectively through the development of self evaluation skills. All the team members felt that working in the team had been informative. It had not always been easy, but they felt that they had greatly benefited from the wide range of experiences and professional understandings that they shared with one another. The teachers expressed a wide range of points, all of which were personal to the individuals involved, and this stresses the need for individual differences to be carefully acknowledged and sensitively responded to. The facilitating role of the project co-ordinator was very important in maintaining a healthy sense of joint responsibility and worth of contribution.

The needs as perceived by all the team members were different. Broadly categorised they were the need for courses on communication with dual sensory impaired children; the need for a broader perspective on a national and international level with regard to all aspects of provision for dual sensory impaired children; the need to develop greater multi-professional and parental links in order to benefit from the contributions that they had to offer. All the members were also aware that a number of needs emerged that could only be identified as the project proceeded.

Important messages from the project team

The team members were asked to indicate the messages that they would like to be noted during the formal evaluation process. They appreciated the two terms that they were being given to ease into the project before the Regional Advisory and Assessment Centre was opened. They welcomed the opportunity to collaborate with colleagues in the LEAs. It was important that their professional development needs were responded to as they emerged, and that the Consortium Steering Committee remained positively supportive.

To develop an effective provision for children with dual impairments of sight and hearing took time as the team explored and developed their understandings. The team felt a strong sense of pride and responsibility for the project and a keen desire to be constructive at all times. During the work of the project it was felt important to remember that it is the children themselves who are at the heart of the project and that at the end of the day it is they and their families who should be seen to have clearly benefited.

Critical points

It is possible to identify a number of critical points that affected the professional development of the project team.

There was a need for a clear public statement about professional expectations of the new service. The setting up of this new service for dual sensory impaired children led to many people having new expectations. There was a danger that these multiple expectations would become impossible to fulfil unless clear ground rules and guidelines concerning the policy intentions and strategy of the project were agreed and adhered to by the Consortium Steering Committee, the LEAs and the project team.

There was a need to be proactive in supporting the project team. With this new high profile responsibility, the members of the team felt that they were in a vulnerable position, having to make provision for dual sensory impaired children but not having completed their own identified professional development. This could have proved counter productive and inhibited the team's willingness to have their thinking challenged. They were also working in a way that was quite new to the region as well as with a group of children who had only partially been identified and whose needs had not been fully recognised. There were many unknown answers to new questions that were emerging as the new provision was explored.

The professional development of these individuals had necessarily to be flexible and responsive as well as taking on board the need to provide a very steep learning curve. Ways of providing this support needed to be identified. In analysing the evidence it became clear that each member of the team had a different set of perceptions of the challenges and that each of them had a different set of needs. These differences needed to continue to be openly acknowledged within the team so that strengths could be worked to and areas of lesser confidence could be both challenged and supported.

The new responsibilities for the project team proved to be very challenging. All of the members felt a sense of pride and responsibility towards ensuring the success of the project and they demonstrated enthusiasm, sensitivity and concern which were commendable. They were eager to learn and add to their considerable professional knowledge and skill.

The professional development of LEA-based teachers and other professionals

There were different levels of support and training for professionals in the region offered by the consortium, these being advice and support for individuals, school and situation-specific awareness raising, LEA-negotiated induction and award-bearing INSET. This involved initiative, negotiation and co-ordination with the five LEAs, the non-maintained special school, other providers from within and outside the region including the Special Educational Needs Resource Centre at the University of Northumbria.

Advice, support and awareness raising

Advice and support were given by the project team in different ways: in the classroom, day nurseries, coffee mornings for parents, and home visits made with members of the project team along with teachers from the school. Advice and support were appreciated by teachers and, as one teacher commented, it was seen as a 'luxury, at first... but only what is needed'.

School and situation-specific INSET was described as 'awareness raising' and took place in a variety of settings for twenty-four individual groups within the LEAs during the first two years. Specific requests were responded to and the groups included professionals in education, social services, health authorities, voluntary agencies, and parents. There is no doubt that this training was successful in achieving its intentions. Sample evaluation questionnaires revealed that more time should be allocated and that future courses should include observations of children and case study material.

LEA-negotiated induction normally took place over three days or its equivalent within the LEA concerned. The training took place in all five LEAs and was delivered by a wide range of specialists from within and outside the region in partnership with the project team, whose involvement in the delivery of these courses gradually increased as their expertise developed. The LEA and the project co-ordinator were responsible for negotiation and recruitment. Attendance revealed a wide range of professionals at different levels of responsibility in education, social services, health authorities, and voluntary agencies. The training reached a wide audience and was well received, with many recipients indicating the need for further training such as working with practical case studies of children; additional therapies; use of specialists to reach a wider audience; and more opportunities for people to visit the Regional Advisory and Assessment Centre, based at the non-maintained special school.

Award-bearing INSET

Consortium-initiated training was described as 'award-bearing' and delivered through a one-year, part-time, part-distance mode of delivery by a university. The cohort comprised of two teachers from each of the five LEAs, the four members of the project team and one teacher from the non-maintained special school. Course members worked in their professional capacity with children who were defined as deafblind but in fact covered a wide range of dual sensory impaired children predominantly in special schools and nurseries. The LEAs approached the recruitment of course members in different ways and using different local-determined criteria to select teachers from different posts and responsibilities. One LEA selected two advisory teachers; one selected an advisory teacher and a teacher in a school for children with severe learning difficulties; two LEAs recruited both teachers from schools for children with severe learning difficulties; and one LEA selected a teacher in a school for children with severe learning difficulties and another in the day nursery of a child development centre run by a regional health authority. The recruitment differed according to local variations in provision but it was felt that this was a positive characteristic since variety created depth and provided a view of the range of dual sensory impaired children.

Only two course members had attended related short courses. Six had attended short courses for the visually impaired, four for the hearing impaired, and two for multi-sensory impairments. One had experienced specific deafblind-related training during an award-bearing in-service course for special educational needs and three had specific inputs during initial teacher training for teaching children with severe learning difficulties. All course members had built up their own ways of meeting the needs of the dual sensory impaired child through close working relationships, in particular with colleagues in school and/or the advisory/peripatetic services. All course members had previously gained a qualification in one aspect of teaching children with special educational needs, nine having qualifications in addition to their initial training, two with a qualifications for teaching the visually impaired and one for both the hearing and visually impaired.

The course successfully met the diverse needs of its course members through a flexible yet structured approach regionally delivered. Course members noted the high level of expertise, organisation, support, and methods of delivery and that there had been a pleasing balance between theory and practice. To many the course was seen as being compact and stimulating, certainly during the first three days. Many welcomed the practical approach during the second period of three days. Assessment was noted as being a positive, prominent feature and course members appeared to have learned much from the experience. Course members welcomed the approach of discussing children as individuals and the course presented new knowledge and skills to the majority of its members, whilst refreshing and updating points of reference to others.

The course members had to complete a final assignment/project which was seen as being very important. The basis for this was that it had to be either service based or classroom based. Topics such as the future developments of a service for deafblind children, a training video for parents, rebound therapy, and teaching strategies were examples.

Within the constraints of a one year part-time part distance mode of delivery the course benefited its members' current work with dual sensory impaired children. All teachers commented upon their development of a deeper understanding of the concerns of the dual sensory impaired child through addressing assessment and observation procedures.

A major feature of the training plan was the building of a network of professionals across the region who would work closely together through the organisation of reading materials and activities. Awareness of the environment and working relationships with advisory and peripatetic services appeared to have been enhanced as a knowledge base had been added to course members' previous experiences. It was also noted that there had been benefits for other children with special educational needs as well as with the dual sensory impaired children. Course members saw specific benefits of completing the course in that they had gained knowledge and understanding of the problems faced by teachers and particularly parents of the children. Specific mention was made of assessment, identification, and skills in classroom management, thereby optimising the learning environment for the children.

Course members reported that they felt increased confidence in working with support staff and were able to pass on information, particularly new-found knowledge on hearing and visual impairments. One teacher commented that the school library had been updated as a direct result of attending the course and two said that there was a movement towards developing school policies.

The participants commented upon opportunities for developing their roles within their LEAs and notably they felt that, within the current climate of amalgamations and reorganisations alongside administrative delays, there may be few openings within the foreseeable future. The majority did not see career enhancement as a possibility but saw themselves using their new-found knowledge, skills and qualification to ensure future employment in the prevailing economic climate. In relation to the change in role of course participants, five stated that their role had changed including gaining promotion; gaining a post of responsibility for children with multi-sensory impairments; obtaining a position in another school for children with severe learning difficulties with responsibility for the sensory curriculum; increasing responsibilities for liaison with other professionals; and obtaining positions with responsibility for teacher support and curriculum guidance. Six teachers reported that their general roles had not changed during the course of study.

The teachers saw the future as being involved in translating their learning experiences into a more effective form of provision for dual sensory impaired and other children and helping parents and professional partners in their working environments. In relation to the education of dual sensory impaired children, members of the course reported that their roles had changed: five became the main reference point for their multi-professional partners; four group members were invited to work alongside others in schools, three being seen as the 'expert' and one saying that they held 'knowledge sought after by colleagues'; two felt that they had become more effective in the classroom. One support teacher stated that more time had been spent in schools for children with severe learning difficulties but at the expense of other commitments to single sensory impaired children. Ten teachers reported that their new roles were recognised by other colleagues, with four stating that they had been approached for help and guidance, although two stated that this had been at a superficial level. For one it had become part of the job description and another was writing the school special needs policy. The enhanced status was welcomed.

Critical points

It is possible to identify a number of critical points that affected the professional development of teachers within the region.

LEAs have approached the project differently by recruiting their staff with different posts and responsibilities and therefore developments differed. The consortium approach to this minority disability has had positive attributes for the region, with the development of a teacher network. Teacher expertise in knowledge and practical skills has been developed within the region but the extent to which this knowledge has been transferred to colleagues, parents, multi-professional partners and support staff has differed within each LEA.

There has been an improvement in practice, including assessment skills and increased knowledge leading to improved teaching styles in the education of dual sensory impaired and other children with special educational needs, which has also reached their multi-professional partners.

Perceived benefits of opportunities created by the consortium

Teachers within the region have benefited from the dual sensory impairment-related professional development offered by the consortium and there have been resulting improvements in practice. The regional provision provided by a consortium approach appears to have been a positive and confidence-boosting way forward for developing expertise with children within this low-incidence disability. There has been improved communication with the introduction of regional resources in the form of a newsletter and a growing network of professionals. Professional development activities are continuing with the introduction of a regional award-bearing INSET course and increased confidence in its members to undertake developmental activities.

A newsletter has been issued once every two months during the project with contributions from professionals within the region. This information was found to be useful and informative in many ways, giving ideas and suggestions as to educational strategies and informing teachers of available courses and resources. This newsletter added to other sources of information consulted by those surveyed that had relevance to the education of dual sensory impaired children, including journals, books, the DFE, local and national organisations and publications from the two universities involved with the project.

Regional network days organised by the project on a termly basis were regarded as being 'very informative' and 'firing us with enthusiasm'. The network has spread beyond the award-bearing course members because of the involvement with and delivery to other professional groups. This has been achieved by utilising different sources on a formal professional basis by regular contact with the project team, including liaison, consultation, attendance at other courses, phone calls, joint assessment visits to schools; on a regular formal basis through attendance at the regional network days; at a communication level through the newsletter; on an informal/personal basis through letters and telephone calls.

A number of teachers wished to continue their studies leading to a further award-bearing qualification and there was overwhelming support for courses of a short-term nature related to specific issues. The four members of the project team had conducted development activities throughout the region with many different groups of professionals. These arose as a result of advertising in the newsletter, publicity material, by word of mouth, through personal contacts, through the project co-ordinator and following discussions with LEAs, schools and other organisations. Members of the project team indicated that this aspect of their role had developed since the beginning of the project. The regular contact maintained through the project helped them to share ideas, resources and expertise; develop effective teaching strategies; offer support and reassurance for individual children and parents. The expertise of the project team has been significantly developed and there has been a consequent growth in confidence as they have developed their expertise which, as one teacher commented, 'is evident in their presentation/delivery,' with pupils, parents and teachers.

The professional development activities conducted by the consortium have stimulated the learning process for its members. There has been a continuation of professional development including the setting up of a regional diploma course in multi-sensory impairment validated by a local university. The new course has been negotiated with the teaching staff at the university and the consortium training sub committee and validated within a modular in-service programme. It involves collaborative activity based on working in partnership with other professionals and extends further than the original course. The new provision has been submitted for formal recognition to meet the mandatory requirement for teachers of dual sensory impaired children.

The education of dual sensory impaired children is now being seen as a priority, with improved classroom environments, improved practice, increased use of appropriate resources, and developments of alternative forms of communication with children. Other children's needs are being monitored more closely. The increased identification of children as being dual sensory impaired has brought educational improvements such as prioritising resources; improved teaching strategies; and an appreciation of the problems faced by the children and their parents.

Thinking back for the future

There can be no doubt that professional development of teachers and others relating to the needs of dual sensory impaired children has significantly increased awareness of those children and strategies that can be employed to improve educational opportunities for them. However, on reflection, there are three key lessons that emerge from this experience that might help others in the future.

A regional consortium approach is vital for low-incidence groups such as dual sensory impaired children. The role of the Consortium Steering Committee was crucial in maintaining a co-ordinated response to professional development for teachers and other professionals responsible for the education of dual sensory impaired children. They had a key role in relating back to their own LEA-based teachers, schools and parents and additionally they had an important role in monitoring 'in the field' developments of the project and its team members and identifying the application of these developments to the development of their own staff. Without their sensitivity and perceived respect, the project would not have had cohesion and as a consequence the professional development activities would not have been viable.

As long as the project was being funded by the DFE there was plenty of demand for the services that were on offer. The development of the regional provision was to them relatively cost free with, in some instances, cover-costs incurred through staff absence being met by the consortium. Whilst there was clear evidence of added value that resulted from the initiative, no attempt was made to ascertain whether the best value for money had been achieved. As the funding period drew to a close it became increasingly apparent that there would be a significant reduction in the opportunities for teachers to attend the professional development provision that had been established. Without adequate earmarked funding from central government the prospects in the medium and long term look bleak, as teachers of more able pupils with special educational needs make bigger demands on the same professional development funds.

In a market driven approach there is the obvious problem that competition leads to winners and losers, i.e. those who generate the most vociferous demand and those whose voice is not heard. Within any LEA meeting the professional needs of teachers of minority groups are likely to be precarious. If the needs of these pupils are to be effectively met there must remain some catalyst that will allow for regional initiation, negotiation and co-ordination of teacher professional development.

CHAPTER 9

Coals to Newcastle: Enriching and Extending Educational Provision Through Regionalisation

David Etheridge

This chapter draws on the experiences of the North East consortium of Local Education Authorities which has administered GEST 29 (14) funding, designated as provision for deafblind children, for the three years of that funding, from April, 1992 to March, 1995. The North East consortium, made up of Cleveland, Durham, Gateshead, South Tyneside and Sunderland LEAs, has been one of eight consortia formed to apply for and develop this government funding and each consortium has responded to that task in very different ways, determined in each case by the peculiar needs of the regions.

This study cannot and does not claim that the model created to meet the needs of these local education authorities is appropriate or necessarily desirable for any other region of Great Britain. Each region has very different starting points created by existing local and regional services, different socio-economic and geographical needs and also different traditions and assumptions in the ways in which it should meet the demands of dual sensory impaired children and young people. However, the experiences of the North East do reflect some of the common problems associated with making a full range of educational provision available to a low-incidence and at the same time very diverse group of children and young people.

Placement of children with dual impairments of both distance senses has closely followed the categories identified by the 1989 DES policy statement (DES, 1989). There are a small number of dual sensory impaired pupils who 'can be catered for in mainstream schools with appropriate support'. It would certainly be an underestimate of the possible handicapping effects of the environmental experiences of these pupils to suggest, as the DES policy statement does, that their degree of impairment is not 'significant' and that they experience 'a very mild degree of hearing and sight loss'. However, it would be correct to observe that these pupils are extremely well supported in mainstream schools by the local education authorities through their visual impairment and hearing impairment support teams. The pupils are small enough in numbers to enable these support services to provide the range of services needed to enable them to demonstrate their abilities and progress educationally.

The first main category of children that the policy document (DES, 1989) saw as being significant in its discrete educational needs was Category (a), 'those whose needs can be met in special schools for the visually or hearing impaired without the need to establish special classes or units'. Although there are no longer any special schools for visually impaired pupils remaining in the North East there are two special schools for hearing impaired children – Beverley School for the Deaf in Middlesbrough, which is maintained by Cleveland local education authority, and the Northern Counties School for the Deaf in Newcastle-upon-Tyne, which is non-maintained. Both schools have experience of working with pupils with dual sensory impairments and the Northern Counties has traditionally provided a regional resource for the whole of the North East region for children for whom it was not felt necessary to make specialist out-county placements at establishments like RNIB Rushton Hall School and RNIB Condover Hall School. There are also well-established units for hearing impaired and visually impaired pupils sited in mainstream schools which provide a high level of support for sensory impaired pupils and in at least one case have successfully supported dual sensory impaired individuals.

Category (b) of the policy statement deals with 'those with little or no intellectual impairment but for whom the schools at (a) above are inappropriate unless they offer special provision'. This has also been provided by the Northern Counties School for the Deaf within its special needs department, or through the same out-county placements as specified above. However, it is when we come to Category (c), 'those with considerable to severe intellectual impairment, who require full-time provision catering specifically for their dual sensory impairment', that we reach the largest number of children who have an impairment of both distance senses or do not have functional use of sight and hearing. Although some children may be provided with a nursery or school place in the special needs department of the Northern Counties School it is likely that they will otherwise be placed in one of the many LEA-run special schools for children with learning difficulties. They are then supported by LEA services for the visually impaired and the hearing impaired who provide a visiting service to those schools. In the case of a pre-school child these support services are also likely to be joined by pre-school and portage services and special nursery provision provided through Social Services, voluntary organisations like Barnardo's, day centre nurseries situated at Child Development Centres or in nursery classes of special schools. The exact form of service varies widely across the region: in two of the authorities, Cleveland and Durham, specialist MSI (multi-sensory impairment) posts exist in addition to the other services outlined above.

One of the major assumptions of GEST 29 (14) funding has been that since dual sensory impairment is a low incidence disability it is not always cost effective for single local education authorities to make appropriate provision available:

> The small numbers and scattered population of deaf-blind children make it unrealistic for an individual LEA to provide a full range of educational and support facilities. (DES, 1989)

This is not a comment on the inadequacy of local support services but rather a recognition of the very special needs of dual sensory impaired children and the specific and resource-intensive needs of this client group. The DES policy statement (DES, 1989) suggested a model for appropriate provision which covered pre-school to adult services. The range is considerable and the consequent service so large with such a multiplicity of staff and resources that it would be difficult to justify financially in a period of intensive and increasing demands being made across the special educational needs continuum on LEA resources. The services dealt with in this chapter, like the client group dealt with in this book, are those for dual sensory impaired children and young people ranging in age from birth to about fourteen years old.

The severity of a dual sensory impairment and the very broad range of children and young people who can be included in this category also have a significant influence on the reality of local support services for single sensory impairments being able to make available the required resources in staffing and equipment. Many of these children deserve a more significant commitment of time than other children with single sensory impairments. There may be comparatively few dual sensory impaired children around but they have more complex needs, particularly when sensory impairment is accompanied by additional learning difficulties. Often a more concentrated and longer commitment is needed. The building of relationships sufficient to enable children to demonstrate their abilities to a support teacher is a time-consuming business and a heavy commitment for sensory support services that are already fully committed to other groups of children. Even where designated posts do exist, and it is significant that they are in the two largest and geographically most diverse of the consortium authorities, additional support has been sought to maintain the desired levels.

What was important from the outset of the GEST-funded project in the North East in examining a model for regional provision was a recognition of the expertise and the value of that expertise in the local education authorities making up the consortium. This chapter is entitled 'Coals to Newcastle' because if the regional service is to survive it must avoid wasteful repetition and replication of existing services. Any regional or even national service should seek to enrich, enhance and extend existing services for dual sensory impaired children rather than to replicate any of these services by setting up a parallel provision. Not only would this be a waste of resources for all concerned but would also lead to a moral dilemma if regional provision does not continue in the long term: GEST 29 (14) funding has been operative for three years and will finish at the end March, 1995.

It would also be true to say that a regional service cannot meet all needs of all dual sensory impaired children. The client group is so diverse that even on a regional basis purely dual sensory impaired children are so scattered and small in numbers that it would be difficult to maintain discrete, age-appropriate peer groups for long-term educational programmes. The DES policy statement (DES, 1989) suggested that one possible model for placements could be in the form of specialist units in designated schools:

> a. a specialised unit for deafblind children within an existing school, where a full range of professional support and specialist skills including that of assessment will be available. Such units are likely to be established on a regional basis, and it is likely that there would be more than one of these in the region, based at different types of school.

> b. other classes within the school where a specialised unit is based. Here the expertise of the unit can support the additional needs of a child within a school for deaf children, blind children or children with SLD or physical disability.

This assumes that designated schools with their own financial management would be willing to develop such a resource and also that

LEAs would be willing to meet the considerable expenses involved in taxiing children significant distances, and/or meeting residential costs, and/or making out-county placements to other neighbouring authorities.

For the great majority of dual sensory impaired children, who have additional learning difficulties, travel to and from a regional centre for any length of time, or even residential provision away from their home and family, is not appropriate or desirable. Often the best and most appropriate placement is the one in which the child is placed at present, or Category (c) of the DES policy statement which comprises 'other schools, with the provision of additional specialist support' – particularly for children with additional learning difficulties (DES, 1989). It would seem better to make the local special school even more special by recognising the needs and abilities of individual children.

Bardwell (1992) emphasised the wealth of local expertise that is available in special schools themselves, requiring in many cases only to be channelled in the right direction:

> Meeting the needs of children with multi-sensory impairments involves developing areas of expertise already existing within the schools I visit, and in some cases introducing new, specialist ways of working. Within schools for children with severe learning difficulties there is a wealth of expertise in early multi-disciplinary assessment and the development of individual teaching programmes. There is also a comprehensive use of early sensory stimulation activities and programmes. However, there is also a need to extend knowledge of communication, visual and auditory skills appropriate to a deaf-blind child.

Most importantly it should be remembered that the main educator of the child, at least during the school day, is the school and any support can only be supplementary to and supportive of that provision: 'Whatever long term success is possible depends upon commitment and support from the staff and not the visits of the peripatetic teacher' (Bardwell, 1992).

One way of continuing to maintain and enrich local support is to provide professional training for LEA sensory support teachers and to other professionals supporting the educational development of these children. Indeed, it seems sensible that even with a regional service of specially trained advisory teachers these sensory support teachers (who are free to schools at the point of delivery), or designated members of the services, should be provided with this training to at least establish a first or, if schools are also provided with this trainng, a second line of support for dual sensory impaired children at a local level. A regional service cannot and should not attempt to work on its own but rather in collaboration and partnership supporting local services.

Bardwell (1992), in her initial observations on her new position as a peripatetic teacher for multi-sensory impaired children in Essex, stressed how vital it is that formal liaison procedures should be established with the Visually Impaired Service, the Hearing Impaired Service and the Pre-School Service. It is also important to point out that any regional service, even if managed by a group/consortium of LEAs, still remains external to these local support services. Bardwell went on to identify specific areas where she could contribute to a partnership with the existing sensory support teams in her authority. These included long-term functional assessment of visual and auditory skills (requiring time that single sensory support services did not have); developing communication skills (specific to the needs of individual children with complex learning difficulties); specialist in-service training; use of specialist equipment such as resonance boards; and modifying classroom environments. Where designated specialist support is not available or cannot be sufficiently committed within the LEA, these areas seem to be necessary services that should be provided at a regional level and brought to bear where needed.

A regional assessment facility is discussed below. As the DES model suggests, equipment, resources, a specialist toy library and literature base are also vital for teachers and parents working with dual sensory impaired children but are expensive, specialist items that an authority would find it difficult to justify in the present financial climate. A central regional resource base that can support local work again seems a proper role for regional provision and forms a component part of the regional resource centre suggested by the DES policy statement (1989). This enrichment of local provision would be of great value even where specialist LEA support services already exist for these children.

Advisory and support teachers working within a single LEA or even working at a regional level must be aware of the importance of supporting the local services rather than working in their own discrete area. The needs of dual sensory impaired children are so complex that it is doubtful whether any one individual would have the range of skills to be able to meet the full educational needs of a child on their own. As Lacy and Ranson (1994) have observed:

> There is no suggestion that specialisms are unnecessary but the greatest benefit for the child is derived only when the relevant skills, knowledge and understanding are shared. Each professional becomes, to a certain extent, a multi-professional.

They go on to suggest that the role of a key worker could be adopted in situations like this and, indeed, this could be a useful contribution to be made by a specialist support teacher for dual sensory impaired children. A key worker within a team is vital in preventing fragmented interaction with pupils. The purpose of this role is not to do more assessing or teaching but to ensure effective liaison with other professionals and parents to avoid misunderstandings, obtuse reports and uninformed judgements. Other professionals take on an advisory and consultancy role. Perhaps a judicious mix of both direct teaching and advisory work is necessary: joint teaching enabling the transfer of expertise from one professional to another, while consultancy time enables the pupils to receive a unified approach (Lacy and Ranson, 1994). The key worker might also provide that important link for many dual sensory impaired children between pre-school and school-age provision to allow resources to be used effectively and give access to a wider range of professional skills, thereby ensuring continuity in the child's educational management.

Dual sensory impaired children are likely to have significant contact with other local authority agencies in addition to education. This is particularly true of pre-school dual sensory impaired children. Recent legislation and advisory documents have stressed the importance of inter-agency provision. The Children Act 'provides for a collaborative and inter-agency approach in the provision of services to families and children' (DOH, 1991), while the Code of Practice (DFE, 1994), following the 1993 Education Act, argues that for identification and assessment of special educational needs 'there must be close co-operation between all agencies concerned and a multi-disciplinary approach to the resolution of issues'. The Code of Practice goes on to say:

> ... many young children will be attending provision made by social services, the health services or the voluntary or independent sectors when concern about a possible special educational need is first raised. Because early identification should lead to a more timely assessment and intervention which in turn should avoid the escalation of a difficulty into a significant special educational need, it is important that any concern about a child's development and progress should be shared at the earliest possible moment.

A recognised regional service for dual sensory impaired children can provide this service and is an immediate referral point for all agencies in relation to a very small but very special group of children. The North East project has had significant and constant contact with Social Services departments and the Regional Health Authority after only two years in existence. Wider dissemination of the availability of such a service and time to allow it to become established will further increase its use. It should also be mentioned here that awareness-raising and professional training are important for non-educational agencies if dual sensory impaired children are to be identified at an early stage and their whole needs taken into account. Also vital is the existence of a very specialised regional agency that can concentrate on the issues of dual sensory impairment, keeping them alive and fresh in the public and professional minds. One of the great dangers of life after GEST 29 (14) is that the high profile that dual sensory impairment has gained will be lost again to more numerous and more immediately comprehensible disabilities.

A regional service as suggested above has a role to play in supporting and advising LEA services and other local agencies, the degree to which this happens depending upon the amount of expertise and time to exercise that expertise already available within that LEA, schools and nurseries where the child is placed. An allied service, which is difficult to provide through existing support services due to the amount of time involved with dual sensory impaired children with additional disabilities, is that of assessment. Both the DES (1989) and Bardwell (1992) have suggested that this is an important area for discrete specialist services for dual sensory impairment and one which can be activated after initial identification by other local services. Precisely what is meant by assessment is a vexed and ill-defined question, ranging from the understanding that it is to do with multi-disciplinary statutory processess with individuals providing educational advice within their specialist areas, to the on-going functional assessment of educational programmes that teachers and other educationalists are involved in every minute of the day.

Specialists teachers of the dual sensory impaired, whether employed directly by an LEA or brought in from a regional service, have an important part to play in assessment of the child's abilities, however it is defined. Indeed, the Code of Practice (DFE, 1994) states that 'all children with special educational needs should be identified and assessed as early as possible and as quickly as is consistent with thoroughness'. The Statutory Instruments (DFE, 1994) relating to the Education (Special Educational Needs) Regulations, 1994, mention children who are both hearing impaired and visually impaired and suggest that, in providing educational advice for assessment, if 'any person from whom advice is sought as provided in paragraph (1) is not qualified to teach pupils who are so impaired then advice sought shall be advice given after consultation with a person who is so qualified'. It is the duty of schools to consult a specialist (DFE, 1994), and a regional advisory service of specialist and qualified teachers has an important contribution to make in supporting LEAs and schools. Again the complex nature of a dual sensory impairment often means that local services do not have the time necessary for such an assessment. As Best has observed (Best, 1994a), 'assessment over time requires experience, professional judgement' and 'not the application of a cook-book test'.

Another role for specialists is in the early diagnosis of dual sensory impaired children as part of a multi-disciplinary and multi-agency team (DFE, 1994). The DES policy statement (DES, 1989) suggested that by the time a child reaches the age of two the LEA should have begun to plan involving parents, medical, educational and psychological personnel, social workers and counsellors associated with specialist units and appropriate voluntary agencies involved in the assessment procedure and parental counselling. Advisory teachers skilled in working with dual sensory impaired children, along with specialist paramedics such as physiotherapists, speech and occupational therapists, will be needed in the guidance team working with the family. This team could also provide advice for other professionals, such as teachers of the deaf or visually impaired who may be working with children with a dual sensory impairment (DES, 1989). The policy statement also suggested the provision of a regional family centre which can concentrate the necessary resources including specially trained staff, parent guidance and support, equipment and a toy library. A nursery or nursery unit would provide for education and long-term assessment.

The regional service suggested above has been providing a valued service for the past two years in the North East Consortium of LEAs through the Regional Advisory and Assessment Centre. Each authority and the schools in the consortium have been able to access a range of services according to their need in supporting and extending their local services. However, the services that have been free of charge for the past two years due to GEST 29 (14) funding will have to be paid for after March, 1995. A valuable regional resource can suddenly become less valuable and, indeed, expendable to schools and LEAs who are facing financial constraints.

Even in the area of assessment, where the recent Code of Practice and the Statutory Instruments appear to require specialist support from a regional team, it is significant that the wording is such that an LEA or school can easily revert to pre-GEST 29 (14) provision. Educational advice by an expert does not mean that the person is required to be qualified as a teacher of dual sensory impaired children. For these purposes 'a person shall be considered to be qualified to teach pupils who are hearing impaired or visually impaired or who are both hearing impaired and visually impaired if he is qualified to be employed at a school as a teacher of a class for pupils who are so impaired otherwise than to give instruction in a craft, trade, or domestic subject' (DFE, 1994). As the regulations stand, this person can possess either the mandatory qualification for teachers of the visually impaired or the hearing impaired (DFE, 1993). With the best will possible, school and LEA budgets are such that if regional specialist support is not free at the point of delivery and a local specialist is not available it seems likely that they will rely heavily once again on the specialists named in the official documentation who are the hard-worked support services for single sensory impairments.

Tony Best has pointed out the dangers of and threats to regional services in Britain by examining the situation in the United States (Best, 1994b). In the 1970s the USA had an impressive regional service for deaf-blind children. Five years ago this had almost disappeared. Developments were a response to the rubella wave of the late 1960s which resulted in a significant growth in services, many of them directly to children, new programmes and new schools. This all came about as a result of the creation of a number of regional centres for deafblind children, established by the government in order to create new services in multi-state regions. Staff training and consultation were provided and a large number of universities started preparing personnel – nine or ten universities graduating ten or twenty students every year.

Best and Mike Collins suggest that there were a number of reasons for the collapse of this provision which are partly specific to the United States but also of relevance to Britain. Before 1974 there was no mandatory education. Not all children were served in schools and schools that did exist were highly selective in the children that they took. Indeed, some children were served by segregated environments away from home where this kind of placement really was not necessary. Collins also suggests that a philosophical shift from specialised, centralised services for special populations to a belief that all children should be served within their local communities – and, some would say, even fully included in classrooms for non-handicapped peers – was also a significant influence. Many deafblind children were being placed in local community schools which did not know what to do with them.

Collins (Best, 1994b) suggests that the integration and 'keep the children in their local communities' movement meant that many deafblind children were widely dispersed within each state, e.g. 200 children served in 170 schools. There has also been a de-emphasis on staff training and a resulting shortage of appropriate teachers and particularly specialised leadership personnel. Most importantly federal government in the United States has placed the responsibility for educational services for every child on the local authority and the local township and therefore 'we are passing along the responsibility to provide a good and appropriate education to sometimes a group of people who have no concept of what that is' (Best, 1994b). Collins also feels that the field of deafblindness is being diluted by people who are trained to teach 'severely handicapped children' and who feel that 'you can serve such child (*sic*) whether they have sensory deficits or not'.

There seem to be a number of problems in directly transferring this analysis to Britain. The first is that deafblind is a word that is used to denote a low-incidence group of children with a dual impairment of sight and hearing and few if any additional learning difficulties. These children are a small group within a low-incidence group of dual sensory impaired children in general. Indeed, many dual sensory impaired children placed in schools for children with severe learning difficulties have not in the past had their dual sensory impairment sufficiently addressed because there have been so few advisory teachers to train and help them. This has hopefully been partially rectified by the GEST 29 (14) initiatives where the training programmes in these schools and nurseries have at least raised the awareness of the staff and parents. It has also created trained and expert advisory and support teachers both locally and regionally to provide this support. As suggested above, integration of these children in special schools is not necessarily a threat but rather a positive advantage for the majority of dual sensory impaired children.

As for professional training the developments in distance learning courses from Birmingham University and the provision of a regional course in the North East from the University of Northumbria might mitigate some of the financial constraints involved in making staff available for full-time courses in other parts of the country. The dangers here are in cuts in central government funding for specialist professional development and the assumption that teachers with the mandatory qualifications for teachers of the visually impaired or the hearing impaired are qualified to teach and advise on the education of dual sensory impaired children without additional training: and that they are available to do so.

Perhaps the most relevant lesson learned from the experience of the United States is that of the problems of post-government funding and the requirement of LEAs and schools to finance their own support on the same scale as during GEST 29 (14) funding. As Collins has observed (Best, 1994b), it is important to have 'a place in the infrastructure, a surface delivery system that will meet the needs of children in local communities'. He suggests that 'we need a team of people in each state who work within regions, who are connected to one another for support, whose job is to support all of the schools within a district in that state'. In other words it is vital that a regional service, supporting local provision, continues to be available. A continuum of services should also be available so that children can be served in local communities and in specialised and centralised schools. 'In order to be able to guarantee appropriate education for every child there have to be alternatives to the local community, when the local community just cannot deliver a quality service and it will help us focus more on what children need, if we can stay focused on what the content of their programmes needs to be, and start honestly asking ourselves the question "in which environment can that best be delivered currently?"' (Best, 1994b).

It is a relatively simple matter to determine the model for a regional service for dual sensory impaired children having had the luxury of generous government funding. However, maintaining that funding in the cold financial light of life after GEST is not so simple. The DES policy statement suggests two possibilities. Although the North East LEAs work very closely and collaboratively it is unrealistic to suggest, as the policy statement does, that different LEAs in a region might provide different parts of the provision and co-operate with one another in planning it. The needs of the LEAs are so different, finances so constrained and there are so many changes occurring in the roles of LEAs as direct providers of services that, although the will is undoubtedly there, the means are not.

A more realistic proposal draws on existing policy when the policy statement suggests that there are already schools, both maintained and non-maintained, which contain the nucleus of what might develop into a network of regional provision. There is no reason why this should involve significant additional expenditure since LEAs would pay for placements on an actual cost basis as with existing school placements. However, no school in the present financial climate, particularly in the non-maintained sector, is likely to make this level of financial commitment without some assurances of sufficient funding being made available. It is unrealistic to expect LEAs to meet the financial costs of increasing their placements to just under two hundred regionally. Most placements, as suggested above, are realistically, educationally and morally appropriate where they are – in local schools. What is important is to find the money to maintain the support for those school and pre-school placements.

Whatever agency a regional service finds itself under it seems that after GEST 29 (14) it will have to be self-financing and no one source of funding would be sufficient to maintain the level of service required. A service cannot exist from day to day and if adequate specialist staffing is to be possible financial stability, at least on an annual basis, is vital. Most of the schools using the service will be special schools which have small budgets, high specialist needs (physiotherapists, etc.) and limited experience in the running of their budgets. A more attractive, and more financially stable proposition than buying in services when and where they are identified and a model that is being explored by other support services, is for the service to be made available to schools and pre-school placements on the basis of an annual service-level agreement with a regional service for a package of services that meets their individual needs, their existing expertise and their purses. Component parts of this package might include:

1. Specialist advice on individual educational plans, annual reviews, individual children and learning environments delivered in schools, nurseries, homes or any other placement.

2. Specialist advice to enable children to make the greatest progress possible and to gain access to a broad and balanced curriculum relevant to their needs.

3. Access to and use of a specially designed Family Advisory Centre and an extensive range of specialist technology and resources which can also be borrowed.

4. Long-term functional assessment in all the environments in which a child might find her/himself.

5. Intensive individual multiprofessional educational assessments, where appropriate, at the Family Advisory Centre to provide additional information as to a child's abilities.

6. INSET.

Additional services can also be made available to health, social services and LEAs in the form of accredited training programmes for professionals and parents, educational advice to support that of local support services, and the use of equipment, technology and other resources. A specialist assessment and day nursery would fill a gap in local provision and would be available for most of the year. Again an annual contract can be drawn up to gain access to these services or bookings can be taken on an *ad hoc* basis. Family support after school, during weekends and school holidays is also a valuable service and can draw on funding from social services, individual parents and charitable trusts.

Work by Bowers (1992) suggests that, no matter how necessary a service might be felt to be, customers are not likely to buy its services unless they feel that it is a quality service. The research has identified the most important factors which will determine a decision to commit resources in this way and, although related to schools, these might equally apply to all customers:

• service members demonstrate high levels of expertise with SEN which

128

are not currently available to schools

- the service is coherently organised to respond to the needs of schools
- the service responds quickly to school's requests for help
- service members work in particular schools in a regular and reliable way
- team members have sound interpersonal skills, diplomacy and tact.

These factors are as much to do with the management of the service as to the form of the service itself. However, the first point is vital if dual sensory impairment is to be recognised as a disability in its own right rather than an extension of two single sensory impairments. Bowers also brings home the point that a succesful service must be seen as a quality service but also a service that is helping to provide quality educational provision in terms of OFSTED.

A specialist regional resource can also attract additional sources of funding from its training potential in the form of specialist placements. However, any specialised regional resource should be involved in research and development activities related to the improvement of the educational progress of dual sensory impaired children. This is an area that Best and Collins (Best, 1994b) suggested as being of vital importance for the development of services and a potentially significant source of funding that will also further the work and professionalism of the service.

Asking the question whether the regional service for dual sensory impaired children will survive after GEST 29 (14) is not a comment on the identified need for such a service but rather on the quality of the service and the financial difficulties that any regional service that supports a resource-intensive client group is faced with. Regional services belong both to everybody and to nobody because outside the charitable sector they have rarely appeared in the field of non-school special educational support. Resources are expensive because they are specialised. The needs of dual sensory impaired children and their families are complex, time-consuming and very individual. However, if the children are to be afforded equal educational opportunities they are vital. After all, since 1970 all children have had the right to an appropriate education and it has been recently recognised that 'provision for all children with special educational needs should be made by the most appropriate agency' (DFE, 1994).

References

Bardwell, J. (1992) 'Can multi-sensory impaired children be supported successfully throughout a large LEA?' *Eye Contact,* **1**(3), 7-8.

Best, A. (1994a) 'Developing and sustaining appropriate provision', in Summerscale, J. F. and Boothroyd, E. A. (eds) *Deafblind Education: developing and sustaining appropriate provision.* London: Sense.

Best, A. (1994b) 'Trends in policy and practice in deafblind services', in Pape, F. W. (ed) *Access to cultur III. Proceedings of the European Conference of the International Association for the Education of Deafblind People.* Potsdam: IAEDB.

Bowers, A. (1992) 'Planning for the future', *Special Children,* 61, 16-20.

Department of Education and Science (1989) *Educational Provision for Deaf-blind Children.* London: HMSO.

Department of Health (1991) *Co-ordinating Services for the Visually Impaired.* London: HMSO.

Department for Education (1993) *Statutory Instrument, 1993, no 543: Education. The Education (Teachers) Regulations.* London: HMSO.

Department for Education (1994) *Code of Practice on the Identification and Assessment of Special Educational Needs.* London: HMSO.

Lacey, P. and Ranson, S. (1994) 'Partnership for learning', *Support for Learning,* **9**(2), 79-82.